NAKED the LIFE

Also by Duncan Banks

Breakfast with God, Volume 1

NAKED the LIFE

Stripping Life Down to Its Barest Essentials

DUNCAN BANKS

GRAND RAPIDS, MICHIGAN 49530 USA

ZONDERVAN™

The Naked Life
Copyright © 2004 by Duncan Banks

Requests for information should be addressed to:
Zondervan, *Grand Rapids, Michigan 49530*

Library of Congress Cataloging-in-Publication Data

Banks, Duncan.
   The naked life : stripping life down to its barest essentials / by Duncan Banks.
     p. cm.
     ISBN 0-310-25608-9
     1. Christian life. I. Title.
   BV4501.3.B359 2004
   248.4—dc22   2004008350

Interior design by Beth Shagene

Printed in the United States of America

04 05 06 07 08 09 10 /❖ DC/ 10 9 8 7 6 5 4 3 2 1

*God, teach
me lessons for
living so I can stay the course*

PSALM 119:33 MSG

CONTENTS

Part 3: Getting Naked with Others

Part 4: Getting Naked with the Needy

Part 5: Getting Naked at Work

Part 6: Getting Naked with Your Money

Part 7: Getting Naked for the Future

THANK YOU . . .

To Mum and Dad, who made memories for me in life that I will never forget. To Steve, who had the same dream as me when others didn't (much of which is expressed in this book) . . . To Tony who taught me how to find naked compassion . . . To Sheila, whose skills never cease to amaze me . . . To Dan, whose infectious desire to serve motivates me . . . To Ian, who is rapidly becoming my soul mate . . . To Matthew, Nathan and Joe, who make me feel like a hero every time I walk through the door . . . To Amy from the big Z, without whom I would never have written a single word . . . To Carolyn, whose naked critique was spot on . . . To Roger for taking me to see some decent football . . . To Leon, whose friendship keeps me . . . To Starbucks, which has been my home away from home for much of this writing . . . To Bob, the person I aspire to become one day . . . To Graham, whose infectious passion makes me see life differently . . . To Joel, the wisest man and sharpest leader I have ever met . . . to the wild bunch at MCF whose contagious community is transforming my life every day . . . And to Debbie, just the best person to do life with – naked or otherwise!

Finally to you, the reader, thanks for agreeing to get naked with me – you are very brave!

If we need models of how to [arouse interest in the sceptical world beyond the Christian subculture], we need only look as far as the Bible. Only 10 percent of the Bible's material, the epistles, is presented in a thought-organized format. The rest contains rollicking love stories, drama, history, poetry and parables. There, humanity is presented as realistically as in any literature.

PHILIP YANCEY (*CHRISTIANITYTODAY.COM*)

Part 1

GETTING NAKED WITH GOD

1

KISSING
IN THE COFFEE SHOP
How to stay friends with God

NAKED LIFE

I love the French language. It is so expressive. It has that certain 'I don't know what' about it. And the French themselves are a nation of great romantics. After all, 'Je t'aime' sounds so much more expressive than our 'Oi Sharon . . . gissa kiss.'

As I write this, l'amour is in the air. I'm supping on a small decaf americano in the midst of a bustling trendy coffee shop just off London's Regent Street. You know the sort of place, where the tea lady has been replaced with a trained barista. A young couple are sitting opposite me. You couldn't get a cigarette paper between them, they are sitting that close. They peck intermittently at each other's lips like hungry birds at a bag of nuts hanging in a winter garden. I wonder to myself if they will display that same affection when they are old and grey and the air smells less of the aroma of freshly ground coffee beans and more of commodes and Sanatageon tablets.

I get to thinking that every man must remember his first kiss and his first car (probably in reverse order). My mind went back to my first kiss. To be honest, no one had prepared me for that moment and, consequently, it turned out to be a monumental disaster, mainly because I missed. I made the mistake of closing my eyes and thereby didn't notice that I had leaned my head the same way as hers. We bashed noses very hard. The bleeding eventually stopped, by which time the moment was gone. Luckily we got the moment back again a few days later. Now twelve years and three kids on, the rest has become history. As I watch these two young lovebirds sitting opposite, I genuinely hope I never lose that same abandonment and romance of my first flush of love.

'But you walked away from your first love – why? What's going on with you, anyway?' (Revelation 2:4 MSG). Can you hear the sadness in God's voice? Maybe there was a time when you promised him everything. Do you remember? Think back to when you first embraced God. You said he would be the leader from now on, not you. Your money, your future, your hopes and dreams, your heartfelt affection and love, your life itself – all his. But now, *What's going on with you, anyway?* You used to talk a lot together about everything, but now it's only in a crisis. You used to read his love letters with a joy and a hunger, but it's been a while since you did that. You used to tell the world about the new love in your life who has stolen your heart, but now there would be nothing to tell even if anyone asked. You used to chase community with other God-lovers, but now church is just a chore.

If that rings true then what am I to do? 'Turn back!' the writer goes on to say. 'Recover your dear early love. No time to waste' (Revelation 2:5 MSG).

HOW TO MAKE IT WORK

So let's agree not to waste any more time. It's been too long already, hasn't it? Here are three ways to kick-start your love affair with heaven again. Three *making-your-life-work* steps you can put into action today that will help you recover your dear early love. You can do it, really.

Step 1. Start over

'What happiness for those whose guilt has been forgiven . . . What relief for those who have confessed their sins and God has cleared their record' (Psalm 32:1 TLB).

One second after you say sorry you can enjoy intimacy with God again. Cool, eh? It's as if you look up into the sky when you shout your confession to God and the tears start to trickle down your cheeks as you see him write 'not guilty' in the clouds. The burden has gone and at last you can push your shoulders back and hold your head up high because forgiveness has come. How do I know it's true? Because it has happened to me more often than I care to admit. So put it to the test now and start over.

Step 2. Take action

'You're cheating on God. If all you want is your own way, flirting with the world every chance you get, you end up enemies of God' (James 4:4 MSG).

Is there a lifestyle pattern that continues to drive a wedge between you and God? Films with the wrong certificate? Websites with the wrong message? Relationships with the wrong outcomes? Labels with the wrong price tags? Whatever it is for you, take action. Unplug, throw out and even run away if you have to. Do whatever you need to do. God is jealous of your love, so don't flirt with anything else. Take action.

Step 3. Phone a friend

'No more lies, no more pretence. Tell your neighbor the truth' (Ephesians 4:25 MSG).

We were never designed to overcome this *making-life-work* stuff on our own. If it wasn't for Leon and Steve who are on my phone-a-friend list, I would fall more frequently and more painfully. They know me. They know my weaknesses. They hold me accountable. The question is, who knows you – who really knows you? If the answer is no one, then phone a friend and make a date to talk.

Don't lose your first love. Making your love affair with God work is not an easy life choice, but you will never regret making it or pursuing it. You'll soon discover it is what you were really made for.

2

TANYA AND HER LYCRA SHORTS

How to keep spiritually fit

NAKED LIFE

When I got back from the gym this morning, I showered, made a fresh pot of coffee and settled down in my study to write this. Before I got the creative juices going, I flicked through my new email messages. The following story was attached to a friend's message. It made me smile, but it also sparked a thought in my mind about a vital part of how we can make our lives work.

> For my birthday, my wife bought me a week of private lessons at the local gym. Though still in great shape from when I was on the university chess team, I decided to go ahead and try it. I called and made reservations with someone called Tanya, who said she is a 26-year-old aerobics instructor and athletic clothing model. My wife seemed very pleased at how enthusiastic I was to get started.
>
> **Day 1.**
> They suggest I keep this 'exercise diary' to chart my progress this week. Started the morning at 6.00. Tough to get up, but worth it

when I arrived at the health club and Tanya was waiting for me. She's something of a goddess, with blond hair and a dazzling white smile. She showed me the machines and took my pulse after five minutes on the treadmill. She seemed a little alarmed that it was so high, but I think just standing next to her in her Lycra shorts added about ten points. Tanya was very encouraging as I did my sit ups, though my tummy was already aching a little from holding it in the whole time I was talking to her. This is going to be great!

Day 2.

Took a whole pot of coffee to get me out of the door, but I made it. Tanya had me lie on my back and push this heavy iron bar up into the air. Then she put weights on it, for heaven's sake! Legs were a little wobbly on the treadmill, but I made it the full mile. Her smile made it all worth it. Muscles feel great.

Day 3.

The only way I can brush my teeth is by laying the tooth brush on the counter and moving my mouth back and forth over it. Driving was okay as long as I didn't try and steer. Parked on top of a Volkswagon. Tanya was a little impatient with me and said my screaming was bothering the other club members. The treadmill hurt my chest so I did the stair monster instead. Why would anyone invent a machine to simulate an activity rendered obsolete by the invention of lifts? Tanya told me regular exercise would make me live longer. I can't imagine anything worse.

Day 4.

Tanya was waiting for me with her vampire teeth in full snarl. I can't help it if I was half an hour late, it took me that long just to tie my shoes. She wanted me to lift dumbbells. Not a chance, Tanya. The word 'dumb' must be there for a reason. I hid in the men's room until she sent Lars in looking for me. As punishment she made me try the rowing machine. It sank.

Day 5.

I hate Tanya more than any human being has ever hated any other human being in the history of the world. If there was any part of my body not in extreme pain I would hit her with it. She thought it would be a good idea to work on my triceps. Well, I have news for you, Tanya, I don't have triceps. And if you don't want dents in the floor, don't hand me any barbells. I refuse to accept responsibility for the damage. YOU went to sadist school, YOU are to blame. The treadmill flung me back into a science teacher, which hurt like crazy. Why couldn't it have been someone softer, like a music or social studies teacher?

Day 6.

Got Tanya's message on my answer machine, wondering where I am. I lacked the strength to use the TV remote, so I watched eleven straight hours of the weather channel.

Day 7.

Well, that's my week from hell. I am truly glad it is over. Maybe next time my wife will give me something a little more fun, like free teeth drilling at the dentist.

Does that get anywhere near your experience of getting physically fit? It's not far short of mine. Did you know that there is on average a 500 per cent increase in gym membership after the Christmas holidays but only 15 per cent of people are still working out come February? Did you also know that getting started is the easy part, but that it's only those who keep on going that get the benefit? You see, a couple of sweaty sessions with a kit bag full of good intentions won't make much difference to your fitness levels. You will need endurance and perseverance when working out even if you don't feel like it, if you are going to keep on top of things physically.

And you'll need these same qualities in your spiritual kit bag if you are going to keep your inner life toned and fresh.

HOW TO MAKE IT WORK

Paul says to his young charge Timothy: 'Practice these things. Devote your life to them' (1 Timothy 4:15 GWT) – this is no easy ride!

The writer to the Hebrews says 'let us run with perseverance the race marked out for us' (Hebrews 12:1) – this is a marathon, not a sprint!

The Corinthian church learnt that they needed to go into 'strict training' (1 Corinthians 9:25) – this is boot camp not a Sunday school picnic!

So let me be your personal *spiritual* trainer today. Let me suggest three motivational and attainable essentials that will help you press on into perseverance and begin to help your spiritual muscles develop to their fullest potential. Imagine me as your coach shouting these encouragements from the touchline as you play the game.

1. No pain, no gain

'Consider it a sheer gift, friends, when tests and challenges come at you from all sides . . . don't try to get out of anything prematurely. Let it do its work so you become mature and well-developed, not deficient in any way' (James 1:2, 4 MSG).

The ability to see trials as a gift will press an enduring spirit deep into your soul. But this is fast becoming a counter-cultural character trait as we become an increasingly disposable society. When a marriage becomes a challenge, we all too quickly walk away. When a friendship becomes a headache, we stop calling. When a job hits a rough patch, we start re-writing our CV over lunch.

I am not sure I will ever reach the state of mind that welcomes life's toughest trials as a great gift, but I know that when I encounter them, the way I view them is key to how I handle them. The way I handle the struggles of life will either mature me or destroy me.

What is your biggest trial right now? Is it financial, relational, vocational or emotional? Maybe it's a temptation you can't seem to shake off or a decision you can't face making. Maybe it's a recent doctor's report or spiritual emptiness that is making your soul sick. You won't have to dig deep to find the answer. It keeps you awake at night and fills your thoughts each day. Remember this: it's the harsh winter weather that helps a sheep to develop a thick enduring coat. It's the constant pounding of the sea that over time turn bits of grit into priceless pearls. And it's the storms in your life that will cause others to be astonished at your maturity. So welcome trials as a gift that can ensure you are not deficient in any way.

2. Train well, don't just try harder

'Everyone who competes in the games goes into strict training. They do it to get a crown that will not last; but we do it to get a crown that will last forever' (1 Corinthians 9:25).

If you want to be a great accountant, a skilled engineer, a ballet dancer or a top athlete, you are going to need to make training a priority. Can you imagine an accountant meeting a new millionaire client without ever having learnt how to manage money? Merely trying harder at that point is not going to make any difference. Or consider 100-metre runners lining up on the blocks without ever having gone into any training. Just wearing the right gear and trying their best is not going to get them to the finish line first – if at all.

Likewise, can you imagine a Christ-follower who plans to develop a vibrant prayer life or an effective evangelism skill just by gritting his teeth and hoping for the best? Crazy, eh? Yet that is how so many of us lead our lives. We just keep on trying harder and it's getting us nowhere. Keeping spiritually fit is about training well.

So how do we do that? Well, you're clearly on the road by reading this book. It demonstrates your desire to 'train yourself to be godly'

(1 Timothy 4:7). Make sure you press these lessons into your daily routine. Talk to others about what you are learning, get into a small group that will hold you accountable, be the first in the queue when your church gathers for teaching and worship, don't stop reading and learning, put your name down for courses and seminars that will spark you on in your learning. Remember that the best translation of the word *disciple* is 'learner' or 'apprentice' – so get those L plates back on and look forward to being a life-long student of the teacher, ready to receive your graduation reward on that glorious day!

3. Dig deep

'It's the diligent farmer who gets the produce. Think it over. God will make it all plain' (2 Timothy 2:6–7 MSG).

I was brought up in the city of London – and a pretty rough part too. If a cat had a tail down our street, it was considered a visitor. So our family doesn't know a great deal about the world of farming. When my son had just started school, he was learning about the different animals in the farmyard. The teacher held up pictures of lots of animals and asked him where we get milk. 'Everyone knows that,' he said. 'Tesco's!' So being a 'townie', I decided to check this 'diligent farmer' one out with an old friend of mine whose family has been in farming for many generations.

I found out that in order to get to the grain harvest you have to go through the following gruelling processes. First plough the field, then cultivate the soil, drill it and roll it, spray it and then finally combine it. Along with rain and sunshine, this is what it takes to grow a field of wheat; the whole process takes nearly eleven months.

Do you see where this is going? The farmer has to have endless patience and has to work hard below the surface of soil before he reaps the reward of his labour. Ask yourself about where most of your life investment goes. Is it above the surface in creating the right visual image, or is it below the surface in creating a depth of character? You might look great when you present yourself at the office or the school gate each morning, but who are you when no one is looking? You might cope well when life is flying high, but what spills out when life crashes in?

Spiritual fitness takes time and real effort. But the good news is that you are not left to your own devices. God's dream from day one has always been to conform and shape you to take on his family likeness (Romans 8:29). He is modelling your character on his own son, Jesus, and won't stop until the job is done (Philippians 1:6). He is like a divine life sculptor, chiselling diligence into your character, hammering self-control into your character and painting love all over your character. What a creation!

3

ASK AT THE FRONT DESK...

How to find out what God really thinks about you

NAKED LIFE

I think animal testing is a terrible idea: they get all nervous and give the wrong answers. But when it comes to the identity test, and we humans find the 'Who are we?' question at the top of the page, it can cause many Christians to break out in a cold sweat searching for the right answer. My aim is that over the next few pages, you will be in no doubt as to who you are and what God really thinks about you.

I love the old news report that told about a visit George Bush Sr made to a retirement home when he was President. He had spent some time talking with the staff on the doorstep of the home whilst posing for press photographs. Then a TV crew followed him into the lounge to meet the ageing residents. That's where it all went wrong. The first elderly gentleman Bush tried to have a conversation with fell asleep. When he came to the next guy, it didn't matter what question the President asked, the old timer just kept repeating, 'I'm 92 years old, you know.' This was not making good TV for Bush. So he spotted a dear old lady smiling away in the corner of the room. With the camera crew in hot pursuit, he scurried across to her, hoping she would be the one to redeem the situation. He shook her hand warmly and, as she smiled knowingly at him, he asked, 'Please excuse me asking, but do you know who I am?' The senior citizen let go of the President's hand, looked him straight in the eye and said, 'No, I don't . . . but if you ask at the front desk – they'll be able to tell you.'

Whether you are an OAP or the most powerful person on the planet, knowing who you are is so very important. Odd though it might seem, even Jesus had to have his identity burned into him on the day of his baptism. As he came up out of the river, the clouds parted in a Charlton Heston style and the proud father reminded his only boy who he really was – 'my son, chosen and marked by love, pride of my life' (Luke 3:22 MSG).

This all sounds nice, but why did God feel the need to tell Jesus that? After all, Jesus must have known fine well who he was. If my dad called me up one day and said, 'Duncan, you are my son,' I'd think he'd been at the funny tablets again. I know I'm his son. I've been his one and only boy for forty years now.

God knew the value of shouting the truth of who Jesus was from the heavens because just a few verses later the devil was trying to undermine his identity. At the end of Luke 3, God confirms Jesus' identity: 'You are my son.' At the start of Luke 4, the devil tries to undermine Jesus' identity – 'If you are the Son of God . . .'

So who are you? It's important to know. I mean, really know. Beyond all doubt. Because no matter how many times God has reminded you about your heavenly parentage, the devil is trying to undermine it with every step you take. You hold a mirror in one hand, a copy of *Hello* magazine in the other, when a rogue thought pops into your head seemingly out of nowhere: *If God really did make you, then why don't your looks match up to theirs?* You slip into some secret sin and you hear a voice over your shoulder: *If you really are God's child, then how can you do such a thing?* You want to serve God like others do and that slippery voice whispers in your ear again: *If God has given you gifts, then why doesn't anyone else see them?*

It's only God's affirmation of who we are that will help us stay on course in those times. But can we ever be sure of our identity? The Bible says it is possible to be sure who we are and it's Jesus who holds the answer.

'It's in Christ that we find out who we are and what we are living for' (Ephesians 1:11 MSG).

HOW TO MAKE IT WORK

So who are we? In a world awash with so many of the devil's lies about who you are, I want to help you make a stand and burn some biblical truth into your very soul. So heads up Christ-follower, here are three things that are true about you right now. No lies, no pretence, just the plain truth straight from the mouth of God. Nail them to your brain today, and they will change the way you live.

1. You are a person loved by God – deeply!

'*What marvelous love the Father has extended to us! Just look at it – we're called children of God! And that's who we really are*' (1 John 3:1 MSG).

You don't have to make yourself lovable to God. He loves you how you are. I did most of my dating in the days before texting and emails so when I wanted to tell someone of my undying love and affection, it had to be done by an old-fashioned love letter. (Debbie still has a shoe-box full of them.)

Ever wondered what God would write to you in a love letter? Maybe it would sound something like this:

Hey you

I ain't ever gonna stop loving you (Jeremiah 31:3). If I collected up all the times I think about you, they would fill the beach at Bournemouth (Psalm 139:17–18). I make up happy songs about you and sing them in the shower (Zephaniah 3:1). I'm your biggest fan (2 Thessalonians 2:16–17). So just you try and stop me from doing good things for you (Jeremiah 32:40). After all, you are the most valuable thing I've got in my life (Exodus 19:5). You know I'll be there whenever it hurts (Psalm 34:18). You can cry on my shoulder for ever (Revelation 21:3–4). I have given up much so we could be together (2 Corinthians 5:18–9). I went bankrupt just to gain your affection (Romans 8:31–32). And I want you to know that nothing can ever come between us (Romans 8:38–39). Come home with me now and I'll throw the most extravagant party you ever did see (Luke 15:7)! You really have stolen my heart with that twinkle in your eye and that beautiful fragrance on your skin (Song of Solomon 4:9–10).

My darling, you are lovely, so very lovely.
From your lover xx
(Song of Solomon 4:1)

Nuff said, eh? Shove that one in your shoe-box!
You are a person loved by God – *deeply!*
It gets better . . .

2. You are made to be like God – uniquely!

'So God created humans to be like himself; he made men and women' (Genesis 1:27 CEV).

It was my mum's seventieth birthday last summer, and I struggled to find the right gift to give her. So instead I asked my dad to dig out all the old bags of photos stored in the loft at home. I picked out my favourites and turned them into a big album of memories for Mum to enjoy. It was somewhat weird looking back at pictures I had never seen before of my parents. Mum was quite a looker in her swimming costume on Brighton beach and Dad . . . well, he looked like me! The family resemblance was obvious and made me feel good. I couldn't have hidden it or run away from it. The evidence was there for all to see – I am a Banks, no mistake.

Men and women, you have an uncanny resemblance to God. I know, I know, it's an almost theologically illegal thought, but it's true. When people look at you, they catch a glimpse of your Father in heaven. Maybe it's not a physical resemblance, but there is something about you that gives away the family resemblance. Maybe, like God, it's your desire for relationships (you know you were never designed for solitary confinement). Maybe it's your creativity (you don't like life to be just functional – look at the way you decorate your home or tend your garden, or even the way you write or paint or play). Maybe it's the spiritual side you have (you have an internal yearning to step beyond the material and to seek meaning and purpose). Maybe it's that you instinctively know right from wrong. Whatever it is, God made you to be like him and you give him a huge amount of pleasure. You are unique. My friend Gerard Kelly expresses it so well in this poem from his book *Rebel without Applause*:

> There's one Mona Lisa
> One Robin Hood,
> There's only one
> QE II.
> Though others share
> The Hundred Acre Wood,
> There's only one
> Winnie-the-Pooh
> And while some spies search
> For a gadgeteer as good
> For James Bond

There's only one Q.
There's only one Nina Ricci,
One Mouse that's Mickey,
And it's tricky,
But there's only one you.
Roses are red,
Violets are blue,
Genetics have proved it:
There's only
One you.

You are made to be like God – *uniquely!*
And better still . . .

3. You are a person filled with God – powerfully!

'The Holy Spirit will come and help you . . . The Spirit will teach you everything' (John 14:26 CEV).

God hasn't left you alone and powerless in this life. The promise is that his helper is with you, and he will teach you all you need to know to live life well.

I love the story about the mother who brought her nine-year-old son to hear the world-renowned concert pianist Ignace Jan Paderewski. He was playing a sell-out concert in New York and she hoped it would inspire her boy not to give up his piano lessons. The young lad didn't want to be there and certainly didn't want to be dressed in his ill-fitting black jacket and bow tie. The well-dressed and seasoned concert-goers muttered their constant disapproval as the little lad become increasingly bored and restless as they waited for the concert to begin. Suddenly, his mum got distracted, only for the briefest of moments, mind you. Before she could do anything about it, her son had sneaked out of his chair, tiptoed down the centre aisle and was climbing up the steps and onto the stage. The chorus of disapproval grew across the packed auditorium as the boy cheekily lifted the lid of the huge Steinway, sat on the master's piano stool and began to play a rather shaky rendition of chopsticks.

'Get that stupid kid off the stage,' shouted an angry security guard as two burly stewards began to climb the steps onto the stage. Meanwhile, Paderewski had heard the commotion from his dressing room, hastily pulled on his jacket and was walking across the stage from the wings towards the boy playing his piano. The audience hushed at the sight of the great man. What was he going to do about this outrage? How was he going to handle the boy spoiling his show? Paderewski came up behind the young lad, knelt on the stage beside him and whispered in his ear, 'Don't stop playing; you are doing a great job.'

As the boy continued to play, the master put his arms around him and began playing a beautifully improvised piece of music based on the tune of chopsticks. And as they both played Paderewski kept repeating, 'Don't stop. Keep on playing.'

As a child of God you may well feel that your life is nothing more than a ropey, childish rendition of chopsticks and no one is going to want to listen to a life like that. But you are filled with the power of God and the master wraps his arms around and says, 'Let's play together.'

Can you hear the voice of his spirit whispering to you now? 'Don't stop. You are doing a great job; keep on playing.'

You are a person filled with God – *powerfully*.

Who are you? Well, now you know – loved deeply, made uniquely and filled powerfully. If we actually began to live like this, with this truth held high, we would be unstoppable. Jesus once described the devil as nothing more than a common thief (John 10:10). His aim in life is to steal from you. He wants to pop round your place when you are asleep, jump in through the window of your heart and run off with a sack load of your peace, joy, self worth and well-being. And before he jumps out into the darkening night sky, he wants to grab a fistful of your identity too. If you hear those slippery whispers again, then look out for the master as he kneels beside you and begins to add his song to yours, producing the most beautiful symphony heaven has ever heard.

Part 2

GETTING NAKED WITH LIFE

WITH LIFE

4

THE MISSING PRESIDENT

How to rediscover a passion for life

NAKED LIFE

Paul Sussman recalls this story in a recent copy of *The Big Issue*, which illustrates that truth really can be stranger than fiction:

In America a man has been imprisoned for illegally opening 4,000 boxes of breakfast cereal. John Weintraub, 34, of Washington, had become obsessed with the plastic models of American Presidents included as free gifts in packets of Happy Morning Muesli. 'I'd been collecting them for two years,' explained Mr Weintraub. 'I had got the whole set except for Thomas Jefferson. I'd bought hundreds of packets but he was never in them. It was infuriating.' So infuriating indeed, that, frantic to complete his set, Mr Weintraub broke into a local cereal factory and proceeded to open every Happy Morning box he could find in a desperate search for his concluding President. Sadly he failed to find one, and, having been discovered by security guards, was arrested and jailed. 'It's OK though,' he smiled, 'because at my first prison breakfast I opened my Happy Morning mini pack and what do you know – there was Thomas Jefferson inside!'

If you could reshape that man's thinking, wouldn't you want to snap that man up on his release to work for you? Who wouldn't want employees with that kind of passion, commitment and tenacity to achieve a goal? Too many of us, however, opt for the easy path in the workplace and we are getting a reputation for it. We avoid any kind of challenge and limit our efforts to the basic daily requirements of the job. The problem for many of us is that this attitude is also seeping over from our workplaces to our homes and even to our churches. This attitude of apathy is affecting the way we parent the kids, take responsibility for running the home, volunteer to serve in the church and even the pursuit of a closer walk with God.

Learning to become a person of passion and commitment is far from being a recipe for becoming a workaholic. It's the secret ingredient for a more Christ-like attitude to valuing others, living well and getting the most from life. It's an attitude that takes us from the drudgery of having to do something to the delight of wanting to do it. Sociologists tell us that the extent to which we find pleasure in our daily tasks determines the length of our lives. Choosing commitment above laziness and lethargy means you will live longer!

Persistence, diligence, perseverance, intentionality and determination – how can you begin to build these essential qualities into your daily life? What steps do you need to take to chuck out the 'just get by' attitude and develop a new reputation for passion in all you do? And what difference will it make to your life?

HOW TO MAKE IT WORK

You may not be able to change the pressures you face at home or the injustice you feel at work or the confusion you feel at church, but there is one thing you can change and change today – your attitude towards them. Below are some practical steps you can take to change your attitude and make your life work at home, at work and at church.

1. An attitude of passion at home

'Work hard at whatever you do' (Ecclesiastes 9:10 CEV).

Leading churches, writing books, speaking at small dinners, large churches or huge festivals are a breeze compared to my wife's main task of running the home. I know because occasionally I have to do it all on my own when Debbie is working nights at the hospital or is away with her family. Has anyone ever managed to work out how to juggle cooking meals, washing up, bath time, book time and bedtime with trying to watch the big game on TV?

Do those you live with think you are mostly lazy or mostly passionate about life at home? What do you need to change in your home life that will begin to build an attitude of passion and delight for the task and relationships home life demands? Here are two simple steps that you could take:

1. Agree to the tasks that you are to be responsible for at home and then do them consistently and excellently – maybe it's putting out the rubbish, doing the washing up, packing the lunches, shopping or cutting the grass.
2. Show an interest in what others do around the home. I have learnt that even though Debbie is responsible for our family finances, it doesn't mean she wants me to dump it all on her and not show any interest.

2. An attitude of passion at work

'And if someone takes unfair advantage of you, use the occasion to practice the servant life . . . live generously' (Matthew 5:41–42 MSG).

Mark Greene in his book *Thank God It's Monday* tells the story of Emily, a small Chinese lady who works at the United Nations.

> One day one of Emily's co-workers, a fairly large lady, wasn't feeling too well. 'Can I get you a cup of tea?' Emily enquired.
>
> 'No,' barked the other rather shortly, 'I don't like the tea here. I only drink camomile.'
>
> Emily left her, quietly slipped on her coat, took the lift down several floors and went down the street to a nearby shop. She returned with a box of camomile tea and gave it in her small hand to this large lady, who immediately enveloped her in a huge hug, exclaiming, 'Emily, I love you!'
>
> Emily replied, rather muffled from the epicentre of this massive hug, 'I love you too.'

When did you last put your coat on and put yourself out for a work colleague? Do others around you consider you to be a person who often goes the extra mile? What could that look like for you? Maybe it's making tea for someone who has never made a cup for you. Or washing up the pile of dirties stacked in the kitchen sink even if no one else knows it was you. How about saying well done to someone who has never praised you? What about going beyond the call of duty and serving an overbearing and overdemanding customer with a smile even if they don't appreciate it?

3. An attitude of passion at church

'The Holy Spirit displays Gods power through each of us as a means of helping the entire church' (1 Corinthians 12:7 TLB).

A recent survey of church volunteers said they offered to serve primarily because somebody asked them to. Conversely, those who were on the sidelines and not volunteering said they felt unable to because nobody had ever asked them.

People of passion and commitment are nothing like this. They don't always wait to be asked before they offer to serve. People of passion get involved. They don't sit on the edges complaining that no one is interested in them. They take the initiative. They call the church office and make an appointment to see the relevant person.

Passion. How about you and God right now? Is there an attitude of passion in your spiritual life? Are you drifting, just getting by? Or is there a passion in your pursuit of him? I urge you to make that choice because Jesus' passion for you is still as strong as it was that day on the cross when he went to hell and back so you wouldn't have to.

5

HOW ARE YOU
WIRED UP?

How to discover
how you really tick

NAKED LIFE

If you knew me, you would know that one word drives me on every day. The future fascinates me. Not that I am a sci-fi freak – far from it. Rather, I have a passion to see future possibilities and drag them into the present. One of the best leadership activities I have ever done is to take the Gallup Organization's *StrengthsFinder* analysis. It's a web-based tool that enables you to find out exactly how you are wired up and, therefore, how you can maximize your gifts and your passions every day. The Gallup Organization asked one simple question to 1.7 million employees working in 101 companies in 63 countries. The question was easy: at work do you have the opportunity to do what you enjoy doing every day? A staggering 80 per cent of people answered no to that question. So most organizations around the world are only truly getting the best out of 20 per cent of their workers. How bored must the other 80 per cent be! How would you answer that question today?

Gallup said they devised this analysis to start a revolution. That was certainly true for me. So revolutionary, in fact, that since I completed the analysis and discovered how God has wired me up, I resigned from the job I had been doing for eight years. I've now moved 130 miles to a position that best uses my God-given strengths and passions. The data showed my top five strengths. Along with *activator* (who asks when can we start), *maximizer* (who insists that excellence, not average, is the measure), *command* (which leads me to take charge) and *competition* (which means I compete to win), my top God-given strength is *futuristic* (which says 'wouldn't it be great if . . .').

I feel liberated since I have taken the time and trouble to discover my God-given strengths and passions. The Bible says each one of us is wired differently, with different gifts and different strengths (1 Corinthians 12:7) and that we are all different so the church will grow strong (Ephesians 4:11–12). Finding out what your God-given strengths are and how God has wired you up is your responsibility. It's worth taking the time to make this discovery so you are able to maximize your life's potential. And just imagine what the church might look like if we all found out what our gifts were and started employing them for the sake of the kingdom. We would be the envy of every business, every organization and every institution in our society. But it begins with you discovering how God has uniquely wired you up.

HOW TO MAKE IT WORK

'He creates each of us by Christ Jesus to join him in the work he does, the good work he has gotten ready for us to do, work we had better be doing' *(Ephesians 2:10 MSG)*.

Here are three practical ways you can begin that discovery and start to experience the sheer exhilaration of being used by God.

1. Get counting the cost

'So I beg you to offer your bodies to him as a living sacrifice, pure and pleasing. That's the most sensible way to serve God' (Romans 12:1 CEV).

If you are going to honour God with your gifts, it will be a sacrifice. I have to warn you that serving God with the gifts he has given you is not going to be a stroll in the park. But I for one would prefer to be in the heart of the action, getting a bit roughed up, as a tool in God's hand, than to stay as a unfulfilled spectator. You see, your unique gift is not a hobby that you keep locked in the attic for a rainy day; it's a life-long devotion to use regularly, sharpen frequently, develop carefully.

And the rewards are huge. Imagine God using your words to bring hope to the lost, using your hands to bring help to the desperate, using your voice to bring music to the sad, using your wisdom to bring advice to the confused, using your leadership to bring direction to a project or using your generosity to change the history of someone's life. I have found no greater thrill in life than knowing the God of heaven has chosen to use me, no matter how big or small the task may seem. What a buzz!

In order to serve God and his church, we have to count the cost. We also have to take a moment to consider how effective we currently are in our service for God. How can we be sure we are using our gifts and reaching our full potential as we serve God and his church? Complete these three questions below to help you find out.

  a. What is required of me in my current role (what are my responsibilities)? Take a moment to list them below:

  1.

  2.

  3.

b. What do I do that makes the biggest impact for the church? (Too many people are working outside their passion and gifts, so what do you do that gives your church the greatest return for your effort?) Again, list them below:

1.

2.

3.

c. What gives me the greatest buzz? What you do needs to have a pay-off for you in terms of job satisfaction. What things do you do in your service for God that gives you the most satisfaction? List them below:

1.

2.

3.

So how do you know whether you are working to your full potential for God? How do you really know if you have found your passion and gifts and are working within them? Satisfaction in your current responsibilities will come if all the top answers to these three questions are the same. In other words, if the responsibilities you currently have match up with what you believe gives the church the greatest reward and you the greatest buzz, then you are on track.

But if you are currently on the PA team and yet the church gets the biggest pay-off when you lead a small group and your greatest pleasure comes from seeing people grow up in Christ, then maybe you need to look again at what your gifts are and how you are using them. The outworking of this exercise will need careful thought, prayer and discussion with others. It could well be that you will have to make some sacrifices to reach your full potential as a tool in God's hand.

2. Get specific

'Each person is given something to do that shows who God is: Everyone gets in on it, everyone benefits. All kinds of things are handed out by the Spirit, and to all kinds of people! The variety is wonderful' (1 Corinthians 12:7–8 MSG).

Notice how Paul writes. He uses phrases such as 'each person' and 'everyone' and 'all kinds of people'. He is trying to make the point that no matter how you may feel, God says you are useful to him because he has given you a gift, *something to do*. Let me ask you honestly – do you know what that *something* is? Have you ever taken the time to work out what that unique gift might be? Here are three empty spaces for you to put down your top three gifts.

My top three gifts are:

-
-
-

Were you able to list your top three gifts in some kind of order? You should be able to – you really should. I honestly believe it is the responsibility of every believer to know what their gifts are. It's not being arrogant; it's wise. Otherwise, we will never be able to serve God as well as we would like and the mission just won't get accomplished.

If truth be told, up to about five years ago I had never thought about this much. In fact, I couldn't have filled it out at all. But since then I have spent a great deal of time, prayer and research working it out, and it has proved an invaluable exercise. It is sad that so many people go through life never reaching their full potential because they have never understood what their passions and gifts really are. It is sad too that so many churches never reach their full potential because they have never enabled their people to discover those gifts and those passions and use them for the kingdom.

Let me give you a kick-start by suggesting some of the spiritual gifts the Bible talks about. Do any of these click with you? Which ones make you wince and which ones make your heart beat faster? Ask your friends what they think. Talk to those in leadership at your church about how you might be able to maximize these gifts as you serve the church.

Handy-work: The ability to get your hands dirty. To build, make, design and construct things that are of use to others. To do practical things that serve others.

Communication: The ability to explain the Bible to others through a variety of media from spoken word to art, design, drama and music.

Leadership: To line people's feet up behind a dream and motivate them to accomplish it.

Giving: The ability to be generous with resources or time, possessions and expertise and to do it cheerfully.

Evangelism: A passion to see those far from God come close and the ability to help them understand what following Jesus means.

Care: The ability to show love to those who are hurting, to give honest encouragement to those who are down and to show warm hospitality.

Organization: The ability to administrate projects and people and the ability to get things done.

This list is by no ways exhaustive, for there are many other gifts such as intercession, wisdom, discernment, faith, tongues and pastoral care to name a few. Researchers with brains bigger and experience much greater than mine have developed a great variety of excellent tools that will help you discover your strengths, personality traits and gifts. So take time to investigate these. Spend some time at the bookshop or library or on the web looking for one that will help you. Do whatever you need to do to make this discovery – study, read, ask, pray and then try them out.

3. Get stuck in

'Moses begged, "Lord, please send someone else to do it"' (Exodus 4:13 CEV).

The truth is, most of us feel daunted when God calls us to put our gifts into action. Like Moses, we suggest God might think about sending someone else. Someone with more ability and experience, someone with more faith and a better hairdo. We feel this way because God rarely calls us to do the comfortable or the easy thing. His call is always a challenge. It will always take us out of our comfort zones. It will always mean slipping off the slippers and booting up for the long, hard trek ahead!

So what's holding you back from getting stuck in? What's keeping you on the sidelines? Is it that you are too busy or that you feel too sinful or maybe that you did it once and made a real hash of it? If you feel weak or inadequate, you are in good company, for this is how Moses felt when God called him to go to the king and set his people free. Jesus felt it when he sweated drops of blood in the garden before the cross. Paul felt it as he was beaten and shipwrecked in his pursuit of his calling. And the good news is that God needs your weak and wobbly knees to hold up his awesome power. Listen to what Paul wrote about his weakness:

'Three times I begged the Lord to make this suffering to go away. But he replied, "My kindness is all you need. My power is strongest when you are weak." So if Christ keeps giving me his power, I will gladly boast about how weak I am' (2 Corinthians 12:8–9 CEV).

God is glad you feel weak. It's the perfect place for his strength and power to find a home. Don't let your feeling of weak inadequacy prevent you from using your gift. How can you use your gift to benefit those at home? How can you use your gift for the benefit of the people in your world who don't know Jesus? How can your gift shine in your workplace? How can your gift be used with those difficult people you rub shoulders with? How can you maximize the potential of your God-given gift in the life of your church?

So how are you wired up? In his book *The Quest for Character*, the author Charles Swindoll writes: 'How easy it is to be "average". The ranks of the mediocre are crowded with status quo thinkers and predictable workers. How rare are those who live differently.'

If you are going to move from mediocrity and live differently, make discovering your gifts and passions a priority so you can move from the 80 per cent who are bored and unfulfilled every day to the 20 per cent who thrive. Become a person who knows how God has wired you up and is pursuing the development and employment of those strengths every day.

6

WHOSE WAISTLINE IS IT ANYWAY?

How to keep your physical well-being a priority

NAKED LIFE

I cut this out of the letters section of yesterday's *Daily Mail* newspaper. It made me chuckle:

> I was relaxing in my favourite chair on Sunday, reading the newspaper, watching the match on TV and listening to another on the radio, drinking beer, eating a sandwich, serving as a cushion for the cat and scratching the dog with my foot and my wife had the nerve to accuse me of doing nothing!

We chortle because it rings true for so many of us. If doing nothing were an Olympic sport, many of us would be gold medallists! The old adage is true that a football stadium is filled with 22,000 people in need of some exercise watching 22 people in need of a rest. This increasingly sedentary lifestyle is beginning to take a toll on our nation's health. The British public health minister, Tessa Jowell, said she was greatly concerned about the health risks of the growing problem of obesity.

There are many reasons why obesity is on the increase, including lack of understanding of what constitutes a balanced diet, poverty, limited access to fresh fruit and vegetables and an increasingly sedentary lifestyle.

The English, like those in other Western nations, are getting fatter. Twenty per cent of English women and 17 per cent of men are obese, according to a recent report by the Department of Health. It shows the proportion of the population now classified as obese has risen by 4 per cent since 1993. Wynnie Chan, a nutrition scientist from the British Nutrition Foundation, said,

> We are tending to creep towards American figures where at least 25% of the population is obese. Part of the obesity problem is dietary and part was due to the introduction of labour-saving devices, like remote controls.

I realize that eating patterns and lack of exercise are rooted in lots of complicated reasons for many people. And the worst motivation I could use to help you make some positive changes is guilt. It may be a powerful motivator, but the truth is that it just won't last. So I don't want to make you feel condemned or guilty. But I do want to raise your awareness of the fundamental importance of good health and then equip you to make some right choices for yourself.

It may well be a shock to you, but how you treat your body is a spiritual matter. Your body and its well-being is very important to God. When he looks down from the balcony of heaven and picks you out of the crowd, he doesn't just see your soul, he sees your body too. He created you with an amazing body and when he finished it, he stood back and said it was *very good!* (Genesis 1:31). That's the understatement of the millennium. Your body is truly incredible. I described some of God's creative genius in the book *Breakfast with God: Volume 1*.

- A grand piano has 240 strings by which the world's finest concert pianist can produce a soul churning melody. But the

human ear that enables an audience to hear these sounds
consists of 240,000 strings.

- A BBC TV camera has 60,000 photoelectric elements, which
can capture any image. But the human eye, which functions
unceasingly in any weather for around 70 years and has
automatic focus, contains more than 137,000,000 elements.
- A top of the range, industrial IBM computer can handle the
equivalent of one neurone of information at a time. But your
brain has as many as 200 communicating pathways meeting
in a single nerve cell or neurone. This means that in your
brain there are 10,000 million neurones, each one serving as
a mini microcomputer.

So how does God want us to treat our intricately designed human
bodies?

Paul challenges the Christians in Corinth on this by asking them:

Didn't you realize that your body is a sacred place, the place of the
Holy Spirit? Don't you see that you can't live however you please,
squandering what God paid such a high price for? The physical part
of you is not some piece of property belonging to the spiritual part
of you. God owns the whole works. So let people see God in and
through your body (1 Corinthians 6:19–20 MSG).

So do others see God in and through your body? The question
must be that if God has given you an amazingly created body and
paid for it at such a high price, how can you avoid squandering its
potential?

HOW TO MAKE IT WORK

Our aim must be to take responsibility for our bodies. It's more than
just watching what we eat; it's about creating a positive sense of physical well-being. Not primarily so as we can look good in the bath-

room mirror but to be able to both live and serve well. So if you are serious about keeping your body a sacred place, try following the three very practical suggestions below. You will find two things you may need to reduce and one thing you may need to increase in order to keep your physical well-being a priority.

1. Who ate all the pies? (reduce)

'You know the old saying, "First you eat to live, and then you live to eat"? Well, it may be true that the body is only a temporary thing, but that's no excuse for stuffing your body with food' (1 Corinthians 6:13 MSG).

Doctors are in no doubt that obesity is linked to serious health problems, such as heart disease, diabetes, gall-bladder disease, arthritis, musculoskeletal problems and some cancers. They say it causes raised blood pressure and cholesterol levels, which can lead to heart attacks and strokes. Would you say you were the right weight for your size? A healthy weight range is based on a measurement known as the Body Mass Index (BMI). You can get a broad idea as to whether your body is at the right weight by calculating your own BMI. Follow the three simple steps below.

1. Work out your height in metres and multiply the figure by itself.
2. Measure your weight in kilograms.
3. Divide the weight by the height squared (the answer to Q1.) For example you might be 1.6 metres (5 feet 3 inches) tall and weigh 65 kilograms (10 stone). The calculation would then be: 1.6 x 1.6 = 2.56. BMI would be 65 divided by 2.56 = 25.39.

Experts generally consider a BMI below 20 to be underweight and a BMI of 20 to 25 to be healthy. BMIs of 26 to 30 are generally considered overweight, while a BMI over 30 is generally considered obese.

It's amazing to think that most of us would never dream of feeding the cat a diet of chocolate biscuits or filling the car with dirty petrol or swapping our children's evening meals with cakes and chips or filling the baby's bottle with Coke. Yet so often we never give a thought to what we put in our stomachs.

There are two ways you can start to get to grips with what food you eat. The first is to find out what you are really eating. Do a food diary for a week. Don't change your diet, just write down absolutely everything you eat and then look back at the highs and the lows. The second is to use that information to make some dietary changes if needs be. Cut down foods heavy in saturated fats: cheese, fast foods, fried food, creamy desserts. The body needs some fat but not in the amounts that many of us take on board. A healthy daily diet option would include regular high-fibre carbohydrates, fish, salads, at least five portions of fruit and vegetables and two litres of water a day. These are the most pertinent 'rules' to helping achieve a nutritionally balanced intake.

So be honest with yourself about your eating patterns. Are you doing fine or are there some things you need to change? I want to honour you as you begin to honour God with your body.

2. What do you mean, walk? (increase)

'You are no longer your own . . . so use your body to honour God' (1 Corinthians 6:19–20 CEV).

No longer your own, eh? So how are you doing at looking after this body of God's that he has given you to take care of? A recent national fitness survey by Allied Dunbar showed that seven out of ten men, and eight out of ten women do not do enough exercise, and these figures are the same in most developed countries.

Exercise is an important part of looking after these highly prized bodies of ours. Exercise increases metabolism, reduces stress levels, decreases blood pressure, maintains good circulation, raises your energy levels and even, according to scientists, improves your sex life! But why do so many opt out? I think a large reason is confusion between exercising to get fit and exercising to stay healthy. Many of us feel that only hard, strenuous training is beneficial to our health. Dr Andrew Smith, writing for the BBC, says:

> There is a well established and growing body of knowledge that shows mild to moderate physical activity is the best way to a healthy lifestyle. If you want to reduce your risk of suffering from coronary heart disease, obesity or mental health problems, then research indicates that you should be physically active. To achieve these health benefits does not require the same intensity of exercise training that is required to become fit. You can simply build physical activity into your daily living through for example brisk walking or cycling.

So it doesn't have to be horrible to stay healthy. You don't have to spend hours in the gym following the training routine of an Olympic athlete just to stay healthy. One commentator recently noted:

> Why pay 50 quid a month to replicate in steel, rubber and chrome what nature has provided outside? If I fancy a walk, I'll stroll to the shops. I will be going somewhere. I won't be pounding away on a glorified conveyor belt, like a hamster on a wheel, going nowhere.

As a guideline, you should aim to raise your heart rate with exercise to moderate levels for at least twenty minutes, three times a week for significant weight loss to be achieved. Here are my top three tips for making this exercising as much fun as possible:

- Exercise with a friend at a pace that means you can still chat and make it an enjoyable experience. Set a regular time and date and keep each other accountable.
- Change your routine often. Use music to motivate you. Don't get bored with what you do. Try changing the venue. Swap walking or running for cycling or even borrow the kids' scooters.

- Use everyday opportunities. Take the stairs, not the lift.
  Park in the car park furthest away from the shops. Leave the
  car in the garage more often and buy a bike. Make sure you
  do something that raises your breathing levels at least once
  a day.

Keeping fit will help your heart, mind and emotions stay strong
for longer. That's a medical fact. So what's stopping you from starting?

3. Me? Stressed? Nah ... (reduce)

'God is a safe place to hide; ready to help when we need him. We stand
fearless at the cliff-edge of doom' (Psalm 46:1 MSG).

Stress can often make us feel like we are standing at the cliff of
doom. But stress in itself is not always a bad thing. We often need
some level of stress to focus our thinking and sharpen our performance. The real problem is that instead of pushing the pause button
after a busy period, we just fast forward straight to the next rush. Like
a pinball machine, we just bounce from one flashing light to the next
until we eventually read 'game over'!

A Health and Safety Committee report found that in Britain from
2001 to 2002, 32.9 million working days had been lost due to work-
related stress or illnesses made worse by work. The report found over
three-quarters of people thought work-related stress was a fact of life.
Dr Simon Fradd, chairman of the Doctor Patient Partnership, said,
'Stress is the second biggest cause of sickness absence days of employees in the UK. It has enormous impact for employees, employers and
society as a whole.'

A business friend of mine told me recently that he never thought
of himself as someone who suffers from stress, though his doctor told
him that stress had been the cause of his soaring blood pressure. No
wonder, really. Besides the daily pressure of running a multi-million
pound business, he had recently struggled through two deaths in the

family in as many months as well as some serious family illness. And to top it all, Christmas had just finished. That mounts up to quite a score on the stress-level scales. He has since begun to change his eating patterns and has started doing some exercise. It was a real wake-up call for him.

So how are your stress and tension levels these days? Do you feel on the edge in your current circumstances? Are you managing to balance busy times with rest and recovery times? Here are three starting points to help you make rest a priority and beat any rising stress levels. Why not give them a go and see if your stress levels change?

- Try to have a good eight hours sleep a night with as many before midnight as you can.
- Try to book holiday dates in your diary at the start of the year and stick to them.
- Make sure you have a full and uninterrupted 24-hour period a week free when you can just play and recharge the batteries.

A final word for the stressed: Resting in God during the tough times has great results. I took my two young boys to their first motor-racing event recently. They loved it. We parked the car in the overflow car park and had a very long walk through the crowds to find our seats. We sat and watched the racing in the warm sunshine. But when the final race was over, the sun disappeared and the heavens opened. It went from heatwave to hailstones in seconds. We were wearing T-shirts and shorts and the more we headed into the wind and the rain, the harder the boys were finding it to keep going. It was getting too much for them. So I picked them up – one on my shoulders and one in my arms. We eventually made it back to the warmth and safety of the car. I was exhausted as I rested five-year-old Nathan onto the back seat. He wiped the rain from his face, looked up at me and said, 'Thanks, Dad – you're the best!' Those five words warmed my heart and made my day. They made all the carrying and struggle worthwhile.

Your heavenly father knows there are times in life when the stress is just too great and, try as you might, you can't carry yourself through to the end – it's just too much for you. It's at those times that God invites you to jump up into his arms and let his strength become your strength. Hold on tight in those times because the storm will come to an end and then you can say with joy, 'Thanks, Dad – you're the best!'

7

WHAT WOMEN <u>REALLY</u> WANT

How to be a real man

NAKED LIFE

If you are a woman reading this book, then please stop at this chapter. Don't be tempted to read the next few pages. Skip right onto the next chapter. It's for your own safety. This is not for your eyes. I am going to be talking man-to-man here and it could get nasty. So stay clear – this one's for boys only.

I have a friend who works in the fashion industry. She is a buyer for a well-known men's clothing store. Her job often takes her to the catwalks of Milan, New York and Paris. She holds the opinion (rather controversially in my view) that men are the worst dressed of the species and that British men are the worst dressed in the world. Naturally my jeans and polo shirts have often begged to differ with her power suits. So recently she sent me this email from a business trip to Italy.

> Duncan, these are the things you and your male brothers need to understand about style. Take it from someone who knows . . .

Yes, Homer Simpson is funny – but not on your tie. And never consider tucking your jumper into your jeans unless of course you are the local vicar. Remember that Donald Duck socks do not reflect your individuality nor the wild side of your corporate facade. They do, however, mean your mother still dresses you or at least you wish she did. Speedos are only acceptable on Olympic swimmers . . . as are medallions . . . and tracksuit tops and bottoms.

Sleeveless t-shirts are ok if you're 17 and can do the running-on-the-spot dance at the drop of a hat and you're a member of NSync. OK? And if your definition of 'new season shopping' is buying the latest Manchester United kit, then please seek professional help.

Unless you own a rap empire, leave the chunky gold and 'ice' in the window of H. Samuel where it can live a long and happy life doing no one any harm. And take it from me, you'll never impress anyone if you put your mobile phone in the mobile phone pocket of your combats.

Oh and one final thing . . . Chinos – fashionable for 6 months in 1989 and that was it.

Rather harsh, I feel . . . but what does it mean to be a real man in the increasingly political correctness of our twenty-first century society? Are we doomed to be forever defined by our clothes or our style choices? Can we ever be who we were made to be?

HOW TO MAKE IT WORK

Let's expose the stereotypes of twenty-first century manhood for the lies they really are. Here are three things so called 'real' men do and don't do.

Stereotype 1: Real men don't cry

'Love the Lord your God with all your heart' (Matthew 22:37).

Your heart is your emotional centre. God says he wants an emotional, heart-to-heart relationship with his sons – and that will mean tears. Maybe tears of joy as your youngest scores the winning goal in the school game, or maybe tears of sadness as you realize the ramifications of a bad life decision. Psychologist Alvin Baraff:

> Girls are taught to honour and understand their emotions. Conversely, boys are encouraged, even forced to hold in and suppress their emotions. There is hardly a man in America today who didn't grow up hearing such admonitions as 'big boys don't cry!' or 'be a man!' These commands form the young boys' reality.

How true is that? I can remember being told by my parents that 'big boys don't cry' and by my church leaders that 'we don't get emotional in church' and even by my teachers that as British men 'we must always keep a stiff upper lip no matter what happens to us'. I am a man and, therefore, I am not emotional.

Hear it from me, boys. It's okay to cry. It's good to allow your emotions to run free at times. In truth you will find others won't laugh at you for shedding the odd tear; rather, they will respect you for your honesty and vulnerability. As a man you too were designed with two tear ducts. Use them and discover that real men do cry! The most potent description of Jesus in the Bible is summed up in two powerful words: 'Jesus wept' (John 11:35).

Stereotype 2: Real men must look like and act like Arnie

'Give me a man and let us fight each other' (1 Samuel 17:10).

As Goliath stands before the men of Israel in his full battle armour with his sharp and heavy sword pointed at the enemy, he looks and sounds just like Arnie in full combat gear, gun in hand saying in his broken German accent, 'I'm back!' Real men, it would seem, are fighters with huge biceps who have no problems impressing lots of women. Their ancestors would go daily into the fields to hunt and kill the wild beast, then bring it back to the cave for the family to eat. Now they fight their way through the morning rush hour to battle it out in the cut-throat corporate world of modern business. Real men never ask directions – they'll get there eventually. Real men never make a doctor's appointment – it will go away soon.

I wonder whether we often spend too much of our time worrying about how manly we look and act. We look to boost our self-confidence by flexing our muscles at work to impress a boss or on the dance floor to impress a prospective date. Yet if we really want to authenticate our manhood, it is less about promoting the image of modern man and more about demonstrating the image of God in the way we live our lives.

My wife and I sat recently with a group of friends from church over a meal and this very subject came up. I asked the women around the table what qualities they really wanted from a man. After the jokes about the looks of George Clooney and the bank balance of Richard Branson, one single girl said, 'To be honest, what I long for in a man is not the boring macho stuff that doesn't really impress but to see them walking strong with God and inspiring me to do the same. Trouble is, I can't find a man like that anywhere.'

So when are you going to move from boyhood to real manhood? When will you become the kind of man whose identity is not shaped so much by Hollywood movies or lads' magazines but more by simply being a son of God?

Stereotype 3: Real men are loners

'The Lord God said, "It is not good for the man to be alone"' (Genesis *2:18*).

The image of the lone ranger jumping on his horse and riding off alone into the sunset is one that has been a model of real manhood for generations of young people. No responsibilities, no schedules, no dependants to tie you down. Even though community and friendship and sharing life with others is how we were designed, very few men ever experience it.

After God had created the first fella he commented, 'It is not good for man to be alone.' Many men plough their energies into their work and substitute work colleagues for real friends. Let's get this one clear: Real friends know your birthday and the names of your kids. They come round to your house and go on trips and holidays with you. Most women enjoy a depth of conversation that leads to a depth in relationship. Most men cover up their vulnerability in their conversations and reduce their chat to the football scores, the weather and the latest office gags. But one day the work will stop and it's not going to be the endless emails and meetings that will have defined your life, but the people you shared it with. So invest in them today with the same energy and passion you give to your working life.

Be a *real* man. So where do you begin in your quest for an authentic expression of manhood? The key must be to invest more in your inner lives and less in your outward appearance. You can start doing that today. Some final advice for the boys:

> So don't lose a minute in building on what you have been given, complementing your basic faith with good character, spiritual understanding, alert discipline, passionate patience, reverent wonder, warm friendliness, and generous love, each dimension fitting into and developing the others. With these qualities active and growing in your lives, no grass will grow under your feet, no day will pass without its reward as you mature in your experience of our Master Jesus (2 Peter 1:5–8 MSG).

8

MY SENSIBLE TROUSERS

What kind of an old person do I want to be?

NAKED LIFE

Three sisters aged 92, 94 and 96 respectively all lived together. One day the eldest sister drew a bath. She put one foot in the water, paused, then called downstairs to her sisters, 'Am I getting in the tub or out of the tub?' The middle sister started up the stairs to help, then paused and called back downstairs, 'Was I going up or coming down?' The youngest sister, who was sitting at the kitchen table having tea said, 'I guess I'll have to help again. I hope I never get that forgetful!' and with that she knocked on wood. She got up, then paused and called out, 'I'll come up as soon as I see who that is at the door!'

This year I turn forty. The other day I tried to pull my socks up to straighten out the wrinkles and found that I wasn't wearing any. I thought I should buy some anti-ageing cream until I found that it had a sell-by date on the tube. I have been reliably informed (although it sounds more like an urban myth) that I will wake up on the morning of my next birthday, which is 30 December by the way, to discover that during the night the fashion fairy had stolen my dress sense. Gone will be my stonewashed denims and into my wardrobe will come the sensible trouser with the elasticized waist. Apparently, I will wander into town and find myself being strangely drawn into the trouser department of Bloaters and Co. – the sensible clothing emporium. Here I will try on a pair of comfy brown polyester and viscose, stain retardant slacks with loafers and long socks to match.

I was also told recently that psychiatrists report three things go when you start to age. The first is your memory . . . I can't quite remember the others. But I guess you know you are growing old when your teeth go out more than you do, and your pacemaker opens the neighbour's garage door.

The stark truth is that for many people, older age can often mean a time of mourning for forgotten dreams and long-lost ambitions. I really don't want to get to my seventieth birthday and harbour a life of regrets, so now seems just the right time for me to ask the question, What kind of an old man do I want to be?

I can be sure that the things I plant deep down in my life today will come into bloom at my retirement party. So I need to be careful what I sow. I know quite a few cantankerous and bitter older people and deep down I always say to myself, *I hope I never turn out to be like them.* I also know older people whom I find myself being drawn to because I just love being around them. It's those people, the Bobs and Eunices of my world, who are mentoring me well in growing older. They have helped me decide what kind of old man I want to be and it's this: the one that others still want to invite out to parties or to football games or the movies; an older man who is still great to have around even if he does wear sensible shoes and roomy trousers.

HOW TO MAKE IT WORK

Someone once said, 'Ageing isn't a choice but our response to it is.' In so many ways we ourselves determine how we grow old. If, like me, you hear the breath of time breathing heavier in your ear, look at these three essential qualities that will keep you out of mothballs for a while longer – qualities that you can begin to plant in your life today that will determine how you will grow old.

1. The essential quality of gratitude

'*I couldn't stop thanking God for you – every time I prayed, I'd think of you and give thanks*' (Ephesians 1:16 MSG).

Never stop saying thank you! We drum it into our kids until it becomes second nature. Even if they will never be seen dead wearing the lovely purple-and-green jumper Granny has knitted for their birthdays, they must still learn to smile and say, 'Thank you, Granny.' But when the boot (or fluffy slipper) is on the other foot and we are the ones in the rocking chair with only the sound of clicking knitting needles to comfort us, then we forget the gratitude lesson all too quickly. We have a pain so we are a pain. We complain constantly about the weather, the food, the price of tea, the family, Anne Robinson (I guess that one's fair enough). And the result is people avoid us and we complain about being lonely.

Learn to create a culture of gratitude in all you say throughout the day. As you wake up, make your first thought one of gratitude. Thank God for the new day afforded to you. Thank him for the health you have, for your family and your friends. Demonstrate that gratitude with a kind word or act, a card or a phone call – just to say thanks. You'll find it so infectious. Others will soon get contaminated with your thankful spirit and you will find a full mailbox, a full daily diary and an even fuller life awaiting you. People just love to be around grateful people.

2. The essential quality of enthusiasm

'*Therefore we do not lose heart. Though outwardly we are wasting away, yet inwardly we are being renewed day by day*' (2 Corinthians 4:16).

Never give up. As a preacher once said, 'Don't get retired, just get re-treaded and get back into action!' Start by making it your life's mission to pour your time, energy, experience and enthusiasm into a younger generation. Don't begrudge their youth; be a part of it. You can leave behind the eternal legacy of a changed life. Someone might just be starting out on the journey you began many years ago now – a marriage journey maybe or a work or spiritual journey – who could benefit greatly from your wisdom and life experience. People from a different generation don't need you to become identical to them (you don't need to listen to their music or wear their fashion if you don't want to), they just want someone to identify with them – and you can do that. Really, you can.

Young people especially are desperate for spiritual fathers and mothers or even spiritual grandfathers and grandmothers – and you could become one. You may have spent many years enthusiastically developing a career and an income for your family. Now it's time for you to use that same enthusiasm to help develop a value system for others that could change their lives forever.

So live your daily life wholeheartedly and watch as others look at you and want to swap boredom for passion and second best for excellence. Continue to love your spouse as enthusiastically as you did on your wedding day and let others learn how to keep romance alive and marriages that last longer. People just love to be around enthusiastic people.

3. The essential quality of hope

'For to me, living means opportunities for Christ, and dying – well that's better yet!' (Philippians 1:21 TLB).

Never lose hope! You can become a highly infectious hope bringer. Listen to the words of the famous preacher D.L. Moody, spoken in New York a few months before his death and read out at his funeral:

Someday you will read in the papers that Moody is dead. Don't believe a word of it. At that moment I shall be more alive than I am now … I was born in the flesh in 1837, I was born of the spirit in 1855. That which is born of the flesh may die. That which is born of the spirit shall live forever!

I love those inspiring words. Such defiance, such confidence, such hope. If you lived every day with that total assurance that death is not the end but only the beginning, it would give everything you do a much bigger perspective. Your financial arrangements would change, your priorities list would be shaken up and your stress levels would plummet. As others around looked on, they would hanker after that kind of optimism and ten minutes with you would see their own hope levels rise off the scale. People just love to be around hope-filled people.

Ageing. The process of getting old is not avoidable, but the process of letting life pass you by can be. Make this moment a milestone on your life's journey that you will look back on when the hairs are bushier up your nose than they are on your head. Today is the day to begin living your life with a culture of gratefulness, a heart of enthusiasm and a truckload of hope.

Part 3

GETTING NAKED WITH OTHERS

9

RICH, KATH, IAN AND LORNA

How to make the right friendship choices

NAKED LIFE

Those four names mean nothing to you but everything to me. Let me explain. I am staying with some great friends who live in a 500-year-old farmhouse in a beautiful English village. They have generously invited my family to stay with them over the bank holiday weekend and are treating us like VIPs. After a great English breakfast my mobile rings. I regret again that mad moment when I downloaded the theme tune to *Blind Date*. It was some friends who were calling. They said they had both woken up early having had me on their minds. They felt they just had to call to see if I was okay and if there was anything I wanted them to pray about. I was overwhelmed to think that they were so committed to me that I was their first thought of the day. To cap it all off, knowing we were moving house soon, they offered to drop everything and come help.

As I pushed the red button to end the call, my phone vibrated a warning to me that a text message had just arrived. It was from another good friend. (Hope you can understand txt spk.)

Hi budy. Bin prayin 4 u as I drove to wrk 2day. Just want U 2 knw U R a top dude in God's eyes. I dn't knw what I wud do wivout your friendship. Just wanted U 2 knw that I wil alwys B here 4 U coz I knw U wil alwys B there 4 me.

I was beginning to think it was all a wind up. I'm not really that nice. So I started looking out for the TV cameras. Like it or not (and I was beginning to like it very much) today was rapidly turning into a 'I Love Duncan Day'. To be honest, it made me feel a little uneasy, but God seemed to be reminding me that my life was far richer than I thought. My friendship account was bearing fruit. I was loaded. Not with cash, you understand – something far more precious than that. I was flush with people, genuine friends who would willingly share their home with me, think of me at the start of a day and take time to text me a friendship greeting. I realized that my friendship account was gaining interest rapidly. Maybe those investments of time I had made in the past were beginning to pay out – and just when I needed it! Little notes, meals together, long phone calls, watching movies and big sporting events, just being there. These little deposits that I had made, built up over time, were now providing me with a guarantee of meaningful, authentic friendships for the long haul.

So how is your friendship quotient these days? Are your investments growing or declining? It's never too late to form strong relational ties that will last a lifetime. In fact, you can start today, but you are going to need to make some wise relational decisions. The friendship market is a rocky road and getting rockier. Here are five potential friendship stealers that will try to upset your relational investments. Be aware of them and you will be better equipped to negotiate them wisely.

1. Mobility

No longer do people grow up, live and work near the family home. A young professional told me yesterday that she has been in her latest job three years and is getting itchy feet again. She is in her late twenties but has already lived in nine different homes and three different cities and done four different jobs. No wonder she finds it tough to plant strong roots of friendship. For many older people lone-liness and isolation is the most potent killer. Ever frightening social statistics tell us that older people in society are unable to get out much. And when they do, they don't feel safe outside their front door – especially if they live in a town or city with a high crime rate.

2. Entertainment

Xboxes, PlayStations and Game Boys are the friends to many younger people. Too much time in front of a TV or computer screen can sooner or later disable family communication. The growth in reality TV shows like Big Brother demonstrate our fascination with other people's lives, but it can easily become a scapegoat for genuine human interaction.

3. Technology

Whilst email, voicemail, chat rooms and web pages can be great ways of keeping in contact with friends far away, they should never become a substitute for face-to-face encounters with people we meet every day. They can often rob us of the gift of relational intimacy. You can't easily spot body language in a text message.

4. Church

It seems for many Christians, Jesus has come to give them meet-ings and give them in abundance. The necessary mechanics of church life can often take us away from genuine and deep friendships with people in the church. We become colleagues rather than friends. If this gets out of balance, we will find that the work we are doing for God can soon kill the work God is doing in us. The end result? Resentment and greater isolation.

HOW TO MAKE IT WORK

Mother Teresa said that loneliness not poverty was the greatest disease in the world today. So, against these growing odds, how do we invest wisely in friendships that will enrich our lives? After all, if we are really pressed, it's authentic friendship that we long for more than anything else in life.

Choice is the biggest part of the friendship process. Below are three friendship choices you will need to make in order to realize your full potential in finding and keeping authentic friendships that will feed your soul and last forever.

1. I will make a choice to invest good time in my friendships

'You are better off to have a friend than to be all alone, because then you will get more enjoyment out of what you earn' (Ecclesiastes 4:9 CEV).

What's the point of investing all our energy in developing a lifestyle and a home whilst leaving little time to develop great friends to invite in to it? We need to make a conscious choice to make friendship building a real priority. Bill Hybels, the Senior Pastor of Willow Creek Community Church, wrote in his best-selling book Making Life Work about the importance of friendship to him:

> In my humble opinion, life loses half its meaning when it is not shared with close friends. What good is a birthday or an anniversary

or a graduation without close friends to celebrate it? What good is a promotion without close friends to rejoice in it? What good is a dining room, a college room, a back garden, a patio or a guest room without friends to fill it?

If I were to ask, could you give me a list of good friends that celebrate with you when life hits the heights and who weep with you when you get to rock bottom? Or do friendships just fit into life as and when? What one step could you take today that will take your most precious of friendships to another level?

2. I will make a choice to find friendships that will thrill me not kill me

'Wise friends make you wise, but you hurt yourself by going around with fools' (Proverbs 13:20 CEV).

Gordon MacDonald's book *Restoring Your Spiritual Passion* is a book that I read and reread year upon year because it helps keep me on track spiritually. It's my annual spiritual health check. He talks about the vital importance of good friendships in helping us to walk well with God and make our lives work, but suggests we need to make wise choices or we will get hurt.

I can think of certain people in my world whose company invigorates me, and when they leave I am full of resolve, ideas and intentions about God, self-improvement and service to others. I can think of other people in my world whose presence exhausts me, and when they leave I am ready for a long nap!

MacDonald talks about friends who will ignite, share and catch our passion in life, and then he talks of those draining people who sap our passion and steal energy from us. We are always going to come across draining people in our world, and we have a responsibility to show them a level of compassion and friendship. However, we must also cultivate significant time in friendship with people who will spark energy in us. How are you doing at finding the balance between those who give you relational energy and those who sap it?

3. I will make a choice to use my friendships to sharpen me

'Just as iron sharpens iron, friends sharpen the minds of each other' (*Proverbs 27:17 CEV*).

I can so often feel blunt as I try and hack my way through the jungle of life. I long to be sharp. Sharp enough to resist temptation, sharp enough to parent wisely, sharp enough to manage my priorities, my anger, my relationships and my finances. But how do I get that kind of cutting edge in my everyday life? More prayer meetings maybe or more Bible studies, worship events and teaching tapes? They can't do you any harm, but this proverb says it's authentic friendship that really makes your cutting edge sharp again.

It's worth remembering that when you sharpen iron, sparks will fly. The same is true of the best kind of friendships. Is it time for you to move out of your friendship comfort zone, where your relationships are lived at a surface level? Is it time to move from having acquaintances to having friends? The toughest question you'll need to ask to prove the real depth of your friendship is, How honest can I be? I am convinced that if we stop brushing issues under the carpet and start facing them together, we will reap the richest rewards after all, 'a truly good friend will openly correct you' (Proverbs 27:5 CEV). Recently a very good friend took a relational risk with us by highlighting an area of our parenting that we're not doing well on. It was painful at first to hear her honesty even though she delivered it so well, but she was right. Since then our friendship has become richer not poorer, and our parenting skills have also gone up a notch. It is win-win all the way!

Friendship. There is a strong biblical principle that says you will reap both what you sow and how much you sow. The same has to be true of friendship. In other words, the kind of friend you are is the kind of friend you will attract. So choose to make a wise friendship invest-ment today by being a good friend to those closest to you. Invite someone around for coffee and begin to get below the surface with them. Try asking them about their lives. Maybe you can begin to open them up and raise your honesty levels together with questions like these:

- What are the biggest challenges you are facing in life?
- What are your dreams for the future?

And then there is the most important relationship of all: What mark out of ten would you give your friendship with God right now and why?

10

I SHOT
NICKY GUMBEL

How to save
a wrecked relationship

NAKED LIFE

No, really I did. I pulled the trigger, the gun recoiled into my shoulder and I shot the man credited with developing the worldwide Alpha Course square in the back. It was a great shot even if I say so myself. No, it wasn't a dream; it really happened. I had been stalking him for quite a while through the thick undergrowth of this remote woodland. He had no idea I was there as I hunkered down behind a burnt-out stump of a tree that had been violently uprooted. I tried to keep my breathing as quiet as I could, but I was sure the boom of my nervously beating heart could be heard as far away as Belgium. It felt like Phil Collins was rehearsing a 'best of' album in my chest cavity. I could feel it coming in the air that night, O Lord ... Nicky took a step closer to my position. I adjusted my mask, wiped a bead of sweat from my eyes and took aim. I'd got him in my sights. As I touched the trigger, the manic squawk of a bird broke the silence of the forest. It was like a scene from an Alfred Hitchcock movie. I squeezed the trigger tight and unleashed my final bullet. At that moment, Mr Gumbel turned away from me and the flying bullet struck him cleanly, right between the shoulder blades. He crumpled to his knees, coming to rest amongst the dead leaves carpeting the forest floor.

It was at this moment that I panicked as the full realization of what I had done began to sink in. He's a best-selling author, a vicar, a trained barrister, the chaplain to Harrods no less, and I've just shot him. He's going to be a little mad to say the least. The green hue of his jacket was turning a crimson shade of red.

My only consolation (and before you call the cops) was that the precision weapon I had been using had been loaded for me by a rather large Northern gentleman called Derek. And the bullets were not made of hard deadly lead but soft squidgy paint balls. And far from being dead, the Reverend Gumbel was simply out of the game. I'd eliminated him.

My success was short lived because as I stood up to gloat, a welt of green paint slapped against my left leg. I'd been shot too. I walked back to base camp with Nicky and a few other Christian leaders who were part of this three-day leadership retreat. We'd all been shot and were out of the game. We mused over our experiences as we walked. One talked of how frightened these war games had actually made him feel and how grateful he was never to have experienced a real war. Another talked of how worryingly enjoyable it had been to vent her aggression when eliminating an opponent. With that in mind, one senior church leader said he thought he might come back with some of the more difficult people in his church and 'blow them to kingdom come'. We all laughed as we ran through mental lists of difficult people in our worlds that we would love to chase through a forest and take a pot shot at. But it is this attitude that's brought marriages, communities, nations and even churches crumbling to their knees for centuries.

So what do we do when there is even a whiff of relational conflict in the air? How do you respond in the heat of life's battle when your spouse is in a rage, your best friendship is cooling off, your colleague is avoiding you or your kids clam up when you walk in the room? Do you dig in and take your best shot or is there a better way?

Paul says, 'As far as it depends on you' (that's 'bending over backwards' talk if I ever heard it). 'As far as it depends on you' (that's 'doing everything possible and then some' kind of talk in my book). 'As far as it depends on you' (get the picture of responsibility now? Can I finish the verse?), 'live at peace with everyone' (Romans 12:18). So no spiritual pot shots aimed at flooring a brother or firing character assassination bullets aimed to hit someone in the back.

HOW TO MAKE IT WORK

These three practical relational guidelines below really do work. They are not my clever ideas but those of Jesus Christ, the greatest relational expert the world has ever known. I find myself having to put them into practice at least once a week. I've learnt the hard way that if I don't, my life would be littered with the wreck of once-precious relationships that could so easily be beyond rescue.

Step 1: Go straight to the other person ASAP

'If a brother sins against you, go to him' (Matthew 18:15 TLB).

If you are anything like me, you'll want to sit and stew on a breakdown in relationship. You'll be playing clever arguments over and over in your mind until you feel like the victor. The last thing on your mind is to get up and go to the other person. But Jesus' advice is that even if you are really hurt or if you think the relationship is beyond repair, the mature thing is not to sit and stew on it alone but to get up and go to them.

Step 2: Go before you bad-mouth them to anyone else

'*If a brother sins against you, go to him privately*' *(Matthew 18:15 TLB)*.

It's so easy to involve other people and thereby assassinate someone before you get to talk in private. I sat with a good friend just recently who had an issue with me that was damaging our relationship. He was right and I had to say sorry, but I was so glad that he started our conversation by saying, 'I've come straight to you Duncan. I haven't talked to anyone else about this.' Our friendship has gotten stronger not weaker because of it. So don't gather a little group around you to vent your frustration, not even for some prayer support. Work it out just between the two of you.

Step 3: Go to get the friendship back on track

'*If he listens and confesses [his fault], you have won back a brother*' *(Matthew 18:15 TLB)*.

This one's all about attitude. Ask yourself why you are going to see this person in private. Is it simply to get your point over and make you feel better, or is it to win back this precious gift of friendship and relationship? Think about your body language. Make every effort to understand how your friend is feeling and what her version of events is. Try asking more questions and making fewer statements.

Beat the breakdown. Your relationships are more important to you in making your life work than any money in your bank account or any possessions in your home. So guard them closely, take good care of them and invest heavily in them – especially when they are in danger – and believe me, you will be rich beyond measure. Who do you need to schedule an emergency meeting with today?

11

TOENAILS IN THE SUGAR BOWL

How to avoid marital breakdown

NAKED LIFE

A very cheeky and apocryphal story . . .

A man driving along a busy London street was deep in prayer. All of a sudden, he said out loud, 'Lord please grant me one wish.'

Suddenly the sky clouded over above his car and in a booming voice the Lord said, 'Because you have tried to be faithful to me in all ways, I will grant you one wish.'

The man said, 'Build me a bridge from here straight to the opulence of the French Riviera so I can drive over anytime I want.'

The Lord said, 'Your request is very materialistic. Think of the enormous challenges for that kind of undertaking. The supports required to reach the bottom of the ocean. The concrete and steel it would take. I can do it, but it is hard for me to justify your desire for such worldly things. Take a little more time and think of another wish – a wish you think would honour and glorify me.'

The man thought about it for a long time. Finally he said, 'Lord, I wish I could understand women. I want to know how they feel inside, what they are thinking when they give me the silent treatment, why they cry, what they mean when they say "nothing" and how I can make a woman truly happy.'

The Lord replied, 'Do you want two lanes or four lanes on that bridge?'

John Gray, the best-selling author of *Men Are from Mars, Women Are from Venus,* makes a very compelling argument. In many ways we are galaxies apart and yet on the other hand we vow to be bed-fellows 'till death do us part'. We long to understand each other better and to live together under one roof forever. We gladly choose to spend our holidays in each other's company, bring children into the world together and make the biggest decisions of our lives with each other.

It's like two happy babbling brooks running gently down the mountainside. Then one day, as the two become one big river, they crash into each other with so much force and energy that the water seems to rage and roar in a white foamy protest. My wife, Debbie, just couldn't understand why I found it perfectly acceptable to cut my toenails at the dining table even if they did occasionally get lost in the sugar bowl – the white water raged. In those early years of marriage, I couldn't understand why the phrase 'my mum cooks them this way' would cause her such grief as she prepared the Sunday roast – the foaming water bubbled and spat.

When we were engaged we would walk and talk in the summer sunshine. She would romantically roll her eyes at me and with equal passion I would pick them up and roll them back to her. We did our dating in the eighties. The era of big curly perms, long skirts and heavy make-up, and you should have seen how the girls dressed! Our favourite TV programme was *Moonlighting* with Bruce Willis and Cybil Sheppard – so romantic. And our favourite song was 'We're in

This Love Together' by Al Jarreau, the guy who sang the theme tune to *Moonlighting*.

As we walked together, hands and dreams intertwined, we would talk of a perfect life of wedded bliss that lay ahead for us. Some married people argued and rowed – not us. We noticed that some couples would stop holding hands as they walked and would sit at restaurants having nothing to talk about – that would never be us. We laughed at any notion that we would have to work at keeping romance alive and every hormone in my body mocked at any suggestion that we would maybe face confusion or misunderstanding at times when it came to our sex life – who were they kidding?

How little did we know then! How much more we have learnt twelve years and three kids later! How much are we ready to learn in the next however many years we will have together?

HOW TO MAKE IT WORK

On that day the vicar said 'dust thou' and I said 'I dust', I wouldn't have believed I'd be dusting ever since. But how do we make marriage work for the long term? How can we wake up next to the same person every day and be glad about it? How can we still whisper sweet nothings even when the ear now has a hearing aid in it? So if your marriage is a row-free zone where every moment is like a romantic scene from a Hugh Grant movie and where there are not enough hours in the day to fulfil your constant craving for lovemaking, then maybe you can skip on to the next chapter. But if, like me, marriage is a constant mix of magic moments peppered with the odd mortar bomb thrown in, then read on. Below you will find three marriage aims designed to combat the three most common things that sociologists blame for marital breakdown – no talking, no sex, no money. I suggest them as one fellow struggler to another.

Aim 1: We will aim to communicate even if it's the last thing I want to do

'For where your treasure is, there your heart will be also' (*Matthew 6:21*).

If we put our hearts into our treasures, then our partner ought to feel like the most important person in our lives because what matters most to us, what we hold closest to our hearts, should occupy most of our attention. If your partner is genuinely the most valued relationship you have, then it needs to become second nature for you to communicate well together.

Unfortunately my noble aims don't always match up to reality. So how can we actually begin to raise the bar on our communication skills and improve our relationship? (If you are new to married life, now is a good time to develop good communication habits. You will need them when children come along and time and energy are in short supply.) Here is a checklist aimed to help you assess your communication skills and keep your marriage healthy. Ask yourself the question, How am I doing on these? Honestly? Then ask your partner how you are doing on these and see if it matches up to your own assessment.

- I show a genuine interest in my partner's day and always give her time to talk it through with me.
- I often suggest we switch off the TV set to talk, or go for a meal or a walk together.
- We plan regular days or weekends away to give us quality time to talk.
- I am more ready to listen than to talk.
- I never bottle my feelings up and always try to be open about my emotions.
- I don't shy away from confronting problems even if it might lead to a heated argument.

- I never sweep issues under the carpet in the hope they will just go away.
- I consider how and when I talk as much as what I choose to talk about.
- I am quick to say sorry when I need to and never hold a grudge.

Let this honest appraisal kick-start you into taking action.

Aim 2: We will aim to have a great sex life, but it doesn't have to match up to the ones in the movies

'Let my lover come into his garden and taste its choice fruits' (Song of Solomon 4:16).

According to research we are supposed to have sex 2.7 times a week, but what does .7 sex actually look like? Couples often ask how often they are supposed to make love, and the answer must be as often as both of you feel like it! For some couples once a day is the norm but for others once a week or so is just fine. Don't let TV, magazines or even the movies dictate your perspective on sex. They are very rarely true to life. So basing our sexual activity on the media's view of sex will only lead to disappointment as most of us will never match up to it. Let me suggest three buzz words to consider. Attention to these will help in keeping the sexual side of your marriage God honouring and as fresh and erotic as it was on those first few nights together.

Communicate

Don't be afraid to talk about your sex life together, even pray about it. If you think you have a greater sex drive than your partner, then talk about it together; otherwise, you will leave them feeling confused and inadequate. Be open in your conversation about what you like and don't like. Make it your aim to know what really turns your partner on.

Experiment

Don't restrict lovemaking to the bedroom – how adventurous can you be in the kitchen or the lounge or even the back garden? And don't restrict lovemaking to night times – why leave it until you're half asleep? I got a text from my wife at 10.00 the other morning. It simply read 'hi sexy fancy a quickie or RU 2 busy?' I replied that I was not keen on egg-based flans at this time in the morning, but when I re-read it, I knew exactly what she meant. Needless to say, I was home in five minutes!

Romance

A 'Say it with flowers' sign was in a florist window. A man walked in and ordered one rose. 'Just one sir?' the assistant inquired. 'Yes, I am a man of few words.' Spend good time and energy in creating atmosphere and in looking good. It gives you time to unwind and to get in the mood. Here are some things my wife and I have enjoyed together. Leaving little love notes in lunch boxes, summer walks, candles around the bath, music, chocolates, massage oils and even some sexy underwear. (You want to see me in a thong – irresistible!) Without pursuing romance in marriage, we are in danger of reducing it to nothing more than two people doing the washing up and paying the house bills. It's been said that men can't get enough sex and women can't get enough romance. So boys, don't always reserve touching for lovemaking, and remember that the aim here is making love not just having sex.

Aim 3: We will aim, as best we are able, to live within our means

'Watch out! Be on your guard against all kinds of greed; a man's life does not consist in the abundance of his possessions' (Luke 12:15).

It's so easy to get sucked in! The strap-line from a recent credit card advert read 'Don't put it off, put it on.' In others words, spend whatever you want to get, whatever your heart's desire, and don't worry about the consequences. The latest figures for the UK suggest that the average couple in debt owes fourteen times their monthly income. In the past ten years of being in church leadership, I have been overwhelmed with couples whose relationships are stressed to the limits because they haven't dealt well with their money. Here are four ways you can begin to get it right as a couple.

Give someone the job

You might decide on joint or separate accounts, but someone needs to do a monthly budget to ensure you are living within your means.

Make money a hot talking point

Make it a rule to talk about the big buys together (we work on about £50) and then schedule in regular times for both of you to get up to speed on where your general finances are. Decide together what you can and cannot spend each month.

Pack away the plastic

So many married couples today are working as hard as they can to pay off mounting credit-card bills as well as the regular household bills. And it's killing them. So be drastic. Don't spend without thinking. Cut up your cards if they are strangling you. Make it a rule to only use credit cards if you know you have the money to pay it back when the bill arrives four weeks later.

Make giving your top priority

Don't wait until you can afford to give, start to honour God now by giving him the first part of your income on the first day of the week to remind you of who should be first in your life (1 Corinthians 16:2). Debbie and I have made this our number one priority from day one, and we have found that as we try to honour God in giving at least 10 per cent of all our income, he always goes overboard in honouring us.

Married life. Here is the classic Bible verse often quoted to newly-weds. I am not sure we are intended to follow its advice to the letter, but the principle is a good one. 'If a man has recently married, he must not be sent to war or have any duty laid on him. For one year he is to be free to stay at home and bring happiness to the wife he has married' (Deuteronomy 24:5).

In other words, we need to take time to grow in love, under-standing and friendship with each other. This is the true key to mar-ital happiness. We must never allow other things, no matter how honourable and worthy they are, to distract us from this task.

12

ME AND WILL SMITH
LEFT HOLDING THE BABY
How to avoid parental neglect

NAKED LIFE

One of my all-time favourite big-screen actors has to be Will Smith.
I have followed his career from his small-screen days as the Fresh
Prince through to his silver-screen performances in *Independence Day*
and *Men in Black*. And believe it or not, I have something very much
in common with Mr Smith. Fame you ask? Nah ... he is a household
name across the globe, and I am a mere legend in my own cul-de-sac.
Fortune? Nope ... he is a multi-millionaire, and I have only just been
specially selected to become one soon – according to *Reader's Digest*.
Good looks? Well, don't write this one off too quickly. One gorgeous,
green-eyed, blond-haired beauty was nestling in my arms just yesterday letting me stroke her cheek and tickle her ears. But then a few
minutes earlier I had given her a worming tablet so what do you
expect? Okay, so I might not match up to Will in terms of fame, fortune and fanciability, but we both share the hardest job in the world.
Not only is Will Smith a Hollywood heart-throb, he is, like me, a dad.

In a recent interview he described his new real-life casting as the
'hardest role of all to play'. I know exactly what he means. In the

interview he went on to give some fascinating insights into the struggle of parenting. The day before his little boy was born, he had bought a state-of-the-art entertainment system for his Hollywood home. It was huge, expensive and with enough gadgets to launch a satellite into space. As he loaded this exclusive bit of kit into his car, the store assistant gave him an instruction manual the size of a small regional library. Just a few hours later, he recalls, there was an emergency call, and he found himself in the delivery suite at the local hospital being handed a little bundle of newly born life. He says:

> I can work out what to do when my new CD player goes wrong, there is even a 24-hour help line, but no one gives you an instruction manual for a human being, so what do you do when it doesn't seem to be working properly – especially in the middle of the night?

Becoming a parent is relatively easy (and, if I might say, quite enjoyable too) but being a parent, now that's the tough job. If you are a parent, you will understand just what Will Smith means when he says parenting is the hardest role of all to play. So hard, in fact, that often we are tempted simply to give up on it and opt for the easy life. Have you found yourself doing this recently? You used to do the discipline thing well, but now you just let them get away with it to save a fight. You used to monitor everything they watched, but now you spend more time keeping the house clean whilst you let them feast their minds on all kinds of rubbish. You used to make them save pocket money or even earn it, now you dish it out faster than a cash machine on Christmas Eve. You used to insist they clean up after themselves – their plates, their toys, their clothes. Now it just seems easier to do it yourself.

So how are you doing with the kids right now? How would they answer if I asked them that same question? Home is an important place for them. It's the place where their values are cultivated, their attitudes are shaped and their beliefs are formed. So it is of vital importance not to give up on it. We may never become the perfect parent, but still we must never neglect our parental responsibility. As a fellow struggler on the road to parenting success, with my parental 'L plates' still attached firmly to my back, I want you to know that you are not alone. As you ask the tough parenting questions, take heart because even the greatest of Bible heroes had to learn the hard way. Rebekah favoured one son over another, which lead to a major family breakdown (Genesis 27). Eli failed to be firm in his discipline and let his sons go wild (1 Samuel 2). David never brought discipline or training to his son (1 Kings 1).

HOW TO MAKE IT WORK

'You must think constantly about these commandments I am giving you today. You must teach them to your children and talk about them when you are at home or out for a walk; at bedtime and first thing in the morning' (Deuteronomy 6:6–7 TLB).

With parenting it is never too late. Below are three steps you can start taking today to avoid slipping into parental negligence. Steps that will help give your kids the values, attitudes and beliefs you so desperately want for them. The house will be empty before you know it, so act on these three very doable things and they might just stop you walking past your kids' bedrooms when they have left home and regret that now it is just too tidy!

Step 1: Say sorry and they will learn to do the same

'If we admit our sins – make a clean breast of them – he won't let us down . . . He'll forgive our sins and purge us of all wrongdoing' (1 John 1:9 MSG).

Hollywood's best advice in the classic romance movie *Love Story* says love means never having to say you're sorry. In my experience as a parent, love means constantly having to say I'm sorry. I am not perfect and I make more mistakes than a Scottish goalkeeper. Maybe like me, you often feel you have gone too far, lost your temper again and been inconsistent in your discipline – and now there seems no way back. But the truth is, your kids want to forgive you. They need your love and are desperate for their relationship with you to be good.

The keyword that may well unlock this fresh start with them is a genuine and heartfelt *sorry*. It's not a sign of weakness in a parent but actually a sign of strength. It will help them to learn to apologize when they have done something wrong and will quickly melt away any icy resentment. (It will also help them to understand how to take the first steps of faith one day by learning that they are not perfect and need to ask for forgiveness from God.) The film actor Robin Williams once commented, 'It's a wonderful feeling when your father becomes not a god but a man to you – when he comes down from the mountain and you see he's this man with weaknesses and you still love him.'

Step 2: Love them unconditionally and they will learn to do the same

'He won't break off a bent reed or put out a dying flame' (Isaiah 42:3 CEV).

Children develop better, learn, play and laugh more strongly when they know they are loved unconditionally. Your love for them might not guarantee their future as the next Prime Minister or the next David Beckham, but it will be an internal reference point for them no matter what life throws their way. So don't only reserve your demonstrations of love for when they achieve something good like grades or goals; learn to show them that you love them for who they are, not only what they might do.

I try as often as I can to praise my boys for their schoolwork or their good behaviour, but last night as I kissed my eldest boy, Matthew, goodnight and tucked him up into his cosy top bunk bed,

I tried something different. As his head hit the pillow, I told him that if they lined up all the seven-year-old boys in the world, I would pick him every time. This morning he came into my room at 6.30 and told me that if they lined up all the dads in the world, he would pick me every time. He had been thinking about what I had said all night long! Priceless. The famous and very wealthy comedian Bill Cosby once noted, 'Nothing I have ever done has given me more joys and more rewards than being a father to my children.'

Step 3: Watch TV well and teach them to do the same

'If your eye is pure, there will be sunshine in your soul' (Matthew 6:22 TLB).

We need to be aware that the minds of our children are being shaped by somebody all the time: school teachers, playground buddies, family friends and sports coaches to name but a few. But the most powerful influence has to be characters they may well never meet, but who turn up regularly in their living room or even in their bedroom – pop stars, cartoon heroes, presenters and actors. It's true to say that most children these days have three parents – mummy, daddy and telly. A recent NOP poll of fathers commissioned by Care for the Family showed that the average father spends less than five minutes a day in one-to-one communication with his children, yet those same children watch an average of three hours of television a day. Your children will probably also spend more time in front of a TV screen than behind a school desk. So we need to watch what we watch and help our children to do the same. That doesn't always mean switching it off (although at times it may do), but it will mean watching with them. One of the most important roles of a parent is to give your child a good value system for life. So it's important to monitor what TV programmes and movies they watch, what books and magazines they read and where they might go with their friends.

It will be impossible to create a childhood for them that is completely free from any dangerous influences, so your job is to help them make good decisions and navigate well through their world of increasingly bewildering choices. This will involve talking through with them what they watch and read and asking them what their reactions to it might be. Then help them understand the value system that is being presented. Remember also that, like it or not, kids do become like their parents, so watch what you watch – especially when your children are in the room.

One final thought: Please don't stop holding hands with your partner. Even through the ever-increasing piles of washing, ironing, dirty plates and even dirtier nappies, make sure your children know that you and your spouse still love each other. Then they will feel that home is a safe place for them to be. The way you both live together will have a powerful effect on the values your children will adopt in life. So keep the romance alive. As somebody once said, the most important thing a father can do for his children is to love their mother. Even if you are bringing up kids alone and are separated from your partner for whatever reason, you can still show honour and respect for them by the way you talk about each other or to each other when the kids are in earshot.

Part 4

GETTING NAKED WITH THE NEEDY

13

JESUS, YOUR PASTOR AND YOU IN THE BACK OF A BOMBAY TAXI

How to change somebody's world somewhere

NAKED LIFE

In his cleverly titled book, *Upwardly Mobile*, my friend Dave Westlake wrote of a life-changing experience he had in a Bombay taxi.

> The cab stopped . . . right outside the Taj Hotel and . . . people approached the open windows to try and sell us goods or to beg. One girl walked up to me. 'Please, Uncle,' she said. Uncle is a term of respect in India. I looked at the girl and saw that she was around ten or twelve, was very beautiful and dressed in a piece of cloth . . . we moved on before I had the chance to get any money out. I turned to my friend and said how beautiful she was. 'Yes,' he replied. '. . . within a year or two she'll probably be a prostitute and then she'll be lucky to make it into her twenties.'
>
> Later on that night . . . I realised I knew who that little girl was. Her name was Jesus. One day I'll stand in front of him and hear . . . 'I was hungry and you did not feed me. I was thirsty and you did not

give me a drink. I was a stranger and you did not invite me in, naked and you did not clothe me.' And I'll say, 'But when didn't I do these things?'

He'll say, 'You were in a taxi in Bombay, waiting for the traffic lights outside the Taj Hotel to change. For as much as you did not do it for the least of these, my brothers and sisters, you did not do it for me.'

I know how he must have felt. How many times have I switched off news pictures of starving children or crossed over the road to avoid walking right past the *Big Issue* salesmen?

Before my first trip to Africa, I was told by a seasoned missionary not to give to the beggars on the street outside the hotel. 'You can't help all of them so it's best not to try,' he said. My travelling companion on the trip was Tony Neeves, the Vice President of Compassion, the child sponsorship agency. For thirty years he has travelled to some of the poorest places on the planet helping the neediest of children. (Compassion sponsors 22,000 children in Uganda alone.) On the first morning of our stay in Kampala, I took a walk with Tony. The streets were littered with the desperately poor, the lame, the blind, the young and the old, all begging for something – anything, to survive another day. Remembering what the old missionary had told me, I pushed my wallet deeper into my pocket.

Suddenly I felt all alone so I looked for Tony, expecting him to be just a step or two behind me. In fact he was a long way back along the street, pouring coins and notes into every outstretched tin or hand offered to him. When he eventually caught up with me, I questioned his actions. Surely after thirty years he had learnt to walk away from this kind of thing. After all, wasn't he doing enough by working with Compassion? Not everyone would have got something. What about the disappointed ones? Isn't it fairer not to give anything at all? His answer was simple yet profound. He took out his last few coins and squeezed them into the hand of a man with no legs who was propped up against a wall. The man muttered something in gratitude and Tony said, 'I made a difference to that one, didn't I?'

I learnt a valuable lesson that hot, sticky morning in Kampala, one of many on that trip. After all, what was I going to do with my spare cash? Buy some postcards maybe? A drink at the airport? A trinket that will end up at the back of a wardrobe somewhere? I learnt that I might not be able to change everybody's world everywhere, but I could change somebody's world somewhere. I also learnt that if I owned anything that I couldn't give away to someone in need, then I don't really own it – it owns me!

The author Ronald Sider notes in his book *Good News and Good Works*, 'The Bible tells us that the holy, loving God we worship has a special concern for the poor, weak, and destitute. Anyone who wants to love and obey this biblical God must share the same concern.'

HOW TO MAKE IT WORK

'The wicked don't care about the rights of the poor, but good people do' (Proverbs 29:7 CEV).

Strong words. How we care about those in our world who don't have any choice but to suffer day in and day out will tell us a lot about the state of our soul. Getting converted *from* our sin is one thing. Getting converted *to* God's purposes is another. If Jesus, your pastor and you were in the back of that Bombay taxi, how might you all have responded to the girl's cry of 'Please, Uncle'? Let's take a look.

1. Jesus and that girl by the Bombay taxi (How does God view the poor – really?)

'The Lord's Spirit has come to me, because he has chosen me to tell the good news to the poor. The Lord has sent me to announce freedom for the prisoners, to give sight to the blind, to free everyone who suffers, and to say, "This is the year the Lord has chosen"' (Luke 4:18–19 CEV).

At this, the unofficial launch of his public ministry, Jesus made his view of the poor very clear. His passion was to bring a new order where the poor would be set free from all oppression and enabled to make their lives work to the full. His life modelled this passion. How many hungry mouths must he have fed? How many emotionally screwed-up minds must he have freed? How many lifeless bodies must he have blown life back into? He didn't run from the desperate poor; in fact, he surrounded himself with them. In an article for the London Institute for Contemporary Christianity, the eminent British theologian John Stott writes:

> Jesus was not afraid to look human need in the face, in all its ugly reality. And what he saw invariably moved him to compassion, and so to passionate service. Sometimes he spoke. But his compassion never dissipated itself in words; it found expression in deeds. He saw, he felt, he acted. The movement was from the eye to the heart, and from the heart to the hand. His compassion was always aroused by the sight of need, and it always led to constructive action. It seems incontrovertible that if we are even to begin to follow the real Jesus, and to walk in his shoes, we must seize every opportunity to 'do good'.

Think back over the past few days. How many opportunities to 'do good' have you seized and how many have slipped between your fingers?

2. Your pastor and that girl by the Bombay taxi (How can the church make it a priority again?)

'They only asked us to remember the poor, and that was something I had always been eager to do' (Galatians 2:10 CEV).

How would your church view that girl in the taxi? Would it feel sadness, cry even and then preach another sermon on compassion? Or would it change everything to help her and others like her? How much of a priority are the poor to your church's mission?

The apostle Paul told the Christians in Galatia that remembering the poor was a priority and that their efforts to help should be done eagerly. For centuries, the church was the main welfare provider, picking up the people who fell through the many cracks in society. It's only in the last few hundred years or so that governments have begun to play their part. In his book *Faithworks*, Steve Chalke describes the church as 'the original caring profession, pioneering welfare before there even were any secular institutions'.

Bono, the lead singer of the band U2, talked in a recent interview about how he views the church's role with those in desperate need.

> I tell these evangelicals in the United States there are 2,300 verses of Scripture about the poor. It is the central message outside of personal redemption, the idea of dealing with the poor. And I'm asking them, where are they? Where are they on this? In a recent poll of evangelical churches, only six percent said they wanted to do something about AIDS. It's unbelievable, the leprosy of our time if you like.

So how can we begin to crack this one at a local church level?

It's got to start with you and me. Here are three suggestions that will help kick-start your involvement in these issues at your church.

Find out

Collect all the information you can about your church's efforts to help the poor. Make an appointment with a leader to talk it through with them. They should value your feedback and passion.

Get involved

Join any groups that meet to consider these issues and use your gifts to help achieve the goal. (Graphic designers can produce leaflets, cooks can prepare fund-raising meals, teachers can educate, business people can network, young people can campaign, builders can give practical help, etc.)

Teach and pray

Make sure the issue of the poor is mainlined into your church's teaching programme and prayer strategy. Talk about it in any small groups you are a part of.

If we begin like this, we will grow in our understanding of the issues, our passion will increase and our vision will become clearer. Others will get infected with our enthusiasm for the poor. From small beginnings the whole thing could mushroom to become a highly effective ministry.

3. You and that girl by the Bombay taxi (How can I do anything about it?)

'Jesus replied, "They don't have to leave. Why don't you give them something to eat?" But they said, "We have only five small loaves of bread and two fish"' (Matthew 14:16–17 CEV).

What would you have done? That girl by the taxi is one thing. But she is just a tiny part of a much bigger problem. How can you do anything about it?

On the one hand, the mountain does seem just too big to conquer:

> 1.3 billion people live on an income of less than 60 pence a day. 840 million people go hungry or face food insecurity. A third of people in the least developed countries are not expected to live beyond the age of 40. 160 million children are moderately or severely malnourished (UN Human Development Report).

Yet on the other hand it seems eminently attainable:

> People in Europe spend more on ice cream each year than it would cost to provide clean water and sanitation for all the people in developing countries (Dave Westlake, *Upwardly Mobile*).

It is so easy to get overwhelmed when it comes to the poor, just like the disciples did when Jesus asked them to feed 5000 plus people with a sardine sandwich. The command was clear: 'You feed them!' The problem was real: 'We haven't got enough!' The solution was simple: 'Just give me what you have and I'll do the rest.' Jesus doesn't expect you to have all the resources to meet everyone's need; he just expects you to give what you have and watch him multiply it.

One way in which I have begun to do this is to sponsor a child through Compassion. His name is Musabe and he is ten and lives in Rwanda. My 18 pounds a month gives him food, education, health care and, best of all, a Christian education. He has become a Christian through the Compassion project and so has his whole family through his experience of Jesus. We write often and he always writes back. A few years ago he wanted to leave school because it was too hard. It was our letters that kept him there and now he is really thriving. He feels like my fourth son – he really does! You get completely involved with these kids. Our boys tell people that they have another brother in Africa. They saved their pocket money last year and sent him a Christmas gift. They were so excited when his thank-you letter arrived and he told them he had bought a goat with the money. (Nathan wants one now too!) I've discovered that I can't change every child's world in Africa but I am changing one, Musabe's, and Jesus is multiplying it.

The poor. We don't talk about them enough. Revival, however, has become the buzzword for many Christians these days. It is the title of many books, sermons and conferences. Worship meetings are awash with pictures of rivers and waves crashing across our land. But we still see so little of it. Maybe we are looking for it in the wrong place? Are the poor and revival mutually exclusive? Is there a connection point? The Bible says there is.

'Give your food to the hungry and care for the homeless. Then your light will shine in the dark; your darkest hour will be like the noonday sun' (Isaiah 58:10 CEV).

I so want the light of the gospel to shine a whole lot brighter than it is now. Don't you? Maybe it's going to take fewer meetings and a lot more meals for the hungry, fewer house groups and more homeless shelters. And the good news is, you don't need lots of resources to do this. Just give what you've got and let God do the rest.

14

BOB MEETS JERRY THE ANGEL

How to find life's greatest adventure

NAKED LIFE

Have you ever met an angel? To be honest, I don't think Jerry was an angel. He was a balding, middle-aged, thick-set, ex-pro American footballer turned theologian. Not a wing or a wand anywhere to be seen, but his presence that evening in our small group was bordering on the angelic. I will never forget the impact of his words that night. He talked straight from the gut about loving life and squeezing every last drop of juice out of it.

It was one of those balmy summer evenings. The curtains gently rippled at the window, ushering in a welcome breeze. Jerry's smile, warm-hearted humility and divine authority struck a chord with all of us as he spoke. No more so than with Bob. On the surface it looked like Bob had it all in life. Great job in the glamorous racing industry, big pay packet, smart house, loving family, cool car and all that on top of his eternal salvation. After all, what more does a bloke need in life? A good life on earth as well as the guarantee of a mansion in heaven. Bob was not known for his vulnerability, but that night

Jerry's words cracked him. This hard-nosed macho man blubbed in front of all of us. Let me précis Bob's question to Jerry:

'You talk about making life work, Jerry, but I have spent my life chasing the dream and still feel empty. I work diligently, invest in my family, worship God and serve in his church as best I can – all the things the preacher tells me I should do, yet still my heart aches for more. Why can't I find the adventure my heart craves? I never imagined life would be like this. When I was in my twenties and fresh out of Bible school, I really did think I could change the world – no, really, I did. But now that I am in my forties, I have forgotten the dream I once chased with such passion. What is it, Jerry? What's the dream to live for now? Where has that wild-eyed adventure gone? I so want my heart back.'

Jerry answered him with questions. He probed Bob about his heart for faith sharing. At first I thought he was off the point until the wisdom of his questioning suddenly came home to me. 'When did you last pray for your friends who are far from God? Which of your friends know you are concerned for their life and their spiritual destiny? When did you last talk deeply about your faith to them, invite them home or invite them to church? When did you last experience the joy overload moment of seeing a friend who was once lost and going to an eternity without God, now get found?' Jerry then concluded with humble authority, 'Honestly, my friend, this is where the real adventure in life lies. This is what you are chasing. This is what you were made for.'

Tears trickled down a number of cheeks that night, not only Bob's, as we sat in prayerful silence. He was right and we all had an honesty moment with God that evening. I was at the front of the confessional queue as we admitted we were once so passionate to see the lost get saved, but that priority had now slipped down the list, nesting somewhere between clearing out the garage and signing up for the church's annual working party.

The action I took with my wife sometime later was to start a small group in our home that we called Curious. We invited everyone we knew (and some we just picked up on the way) who had questions. They came and set the agenda each week and all we did was provide the coffee and the chocolate hobnobs (along with a few pointers about life with God from our experience). The result for us was amazing. It is no understatement to say that having friends like this in our home every week and getting elbow deep in their lives has been our greatest adventure over the past few years. I have never prayed with such a passion as I have watched these people edge closer to the kingdom. So imagine my delight when this message arrived in my inbox just a few days ago:

> As you won't be around for house group for the next two weeks and I am away visiting family over the next two weekends, I have decided to mail you as I didn't want to wait until the end of April when I'll next see you both. On Sunday night I asked God into my life and became a Christian. I just wanted to say thanks for helping me along the first part of the journey. Being part of the house group and speaking with other Christians over the past few months has helped me enormously. I've felt happier & calmer over the last week than I have done in a while and things are more in perspective now. So thanks.

This is the mission, the task, the adventure of life that our commanding officer, Jesus Christ, has called us to. '[He] changed us from enemies into his friends and gave us the task of making others his friends also' (2 Corinthians 5:18 TEV).

HOW TO MAKE IT WORK

Does your heart sometimes beat like Bob's did? Have you lost the sense of adventure you once felt when you first signed up? How can you recapture the wild-eyed enthusiasm of your God-given mission to make lost people friends with him again?

Below are two 'I wills' and one 'I won't'. Three essentials that we must hold dear every day if we are ever going to see this adventure unfold in our lives again.

1. I will make my friends my responsibility

'You must warn them so they may live. If you don't speak out to warn the wicked to stop their evil ways, they will die in their sin. But I will hold you responsible for their death' (Ezekiel 3:18 NCV).

These are tough words, I know, but don't feel guilty – feel motivated. It's not your job to save them – that's where God comes in. It's your job to speak out and you can do this. Remember that you might well be the only Christian your neighbours, or school friends or work colleagues will ever get to know. Don't leave it to someone else to take responsibility. Pray for them, get to know them better, invite them round for coffee or lunch or for a beer to watch the next big game. Then invite them to a suitable event where someone is explaining the story of Jesus in a relevant way. This is where the adventure lies. After all, what's the worst thing that could happen? Christians in the first century were burnt at the stake for speaking out, but the worst that could happen to you is a simple 'No thanks.' So what are you worried about?

2. I will live well, speak nicely and always be ready

'Be ready to speak up and tell anyone who asks why you're living the way you are, and always with the utmost courtesy' (1 Peter 3:15 MSG).

The best way to be ready is to be trained. My wife has been an intensive care baby nurse for over twelve years. She has just completed a new course that will enable her to help save the lives of babies who are born not breathing. Her first shift with this new training was a nerve-racking affair, but she did well and had confidence because of the excellent training she was given.

Maybe you lack confidence in being ready to explain the way you live for God. Well, the best way to be ready is to be trained. After all, if something is worth doing, then it is worth doing better and you only get better by being well trained. Do whatever you can to be ready because it seems to me that God brings people who are lost to people who are ready. What would you say if a neighbour asks you today to explain the difference God can make to her life? Are you ready? Go on a course, read a recommended book, spend time with people who are already sharp on this. So what are you reading to get you ready?

3. I won't beat myself up about it

'The word has gotten around. Your lives are echoing the Master's Word . . . The news of your faith in God is out. We don't even have to say anything anymore – you're the message!' (1 Thessalonians 1:8 MSG).

The word is getting around about your faith in God. You are doing a great job. If you ever hear a preacher shout from the pulpit that Jesus wants you to go into the world tomorrow and *be* salt or *be* light, you can tell him from me that that is who you already are (Matthew 5:16). Sure, your salty flavour can lose it saltiness and become worthless, and your light can lose its brightness. (That's why we need to live well with God and keep short accounts with him.) But if Jesus lives in you, then you already are the salt that brings flavour to a tasteless world and light that brings direction to a lost generation scrabbling around in the darkness. That's who you are. So go with your head held high today and be who you already are. What are you waiting for?

Faith sharing. Life is too short to miss out on its greatest adventure. Bill Hybels, who has been a huge inspiration to me when it comes to this subject, has built his life and his church on the value that lost people matter to God and, therefore, they should matter to us. That's the talk of an adventurer who knows that nothing makes him or his God happier than when someone who is lost gets found.

'Make the most of your chances to tell others the Good News. Be wise in all your contacts with them' (Colossians 4:5 TLB).

15

STARK TRUTH IN THE TURBINE ROOM

How to fall in love with the church (and make others fall in love with it too)

NAKED LIFE

Have you ever imagined a world that had a church that really thrived and not just simply survived? What would that church actually look like? I must confess (unfashionable though it may be) that I have an unbridled passion for the church. I love it. I have made Jesus and his church my vocation and my life's mission. I have read scores of books about the church, debated countless models of effective churches, listened to hours and hours of talks about the church, started a church from scratch and visited many churches around the globe. So when someone talks about church, the precious bride of Christ of which I am a part, my heart leaps.

Yesterday, however, my leaping heart took a knock.

The tube train was crowded and I couldn't get a seat. But no matter, I was so excited about seeing my old friend Tony again. We hadn't seen each other since we had travelled to Uganda together two years ago. We had arranged to meet at the famous Turbine Room restaurant in London. It is beautifully situated high above the Thames in the Tate Modern building, and we had a few hours together before he flew off to Italy to speak at a conference. The conversation, laughter and great stories spilled out as we shared a meal while looking out at an inspirational London skyline. We talked about family, about memories, about new experiences – and about the church.

The last time we met he had been on the leadership team of his church but had grown increasingly disillusioned about what he considered trivialities that were diverting the church from her mission to make a difference in the world. I wanted to know how it was all going now. He had made some positive suggestions as to how they might once again engage their community and arrest the decline. As he presented these ideas of making the church more inclusive, an influential 'old schooler' successfully poured buckets of cold water on his enthusiasm. The old man shrugged off Tony's new ideas and suggested a three-point plan to make the church a better place. First, improve the coffee. Second, reduce the sermons to five minutes and third, stick to the old hymns that everybody knows. My friend left with a heavy heart, balancing his love for the church with his fear for her future. All I could do was to remind him that Jesus once described his church as 'so expansive with energy that not even the gates of hell will be able to keep it out' (Matthew 16:18 MSG).

The train journey home was just as crowded, but I managed to get a seat by the window. As the train pulled out of Marylebone Station and I settled down to read the *London Evening Standard*, my phone rang. It was another good friend of mine, a church leader who also has a passion for the church he leads. He had just been to a conference by an eminent author and commentator on church and how it relates to society.

'How was it?' I asked, expecting him to have had a great day learning and growing in his understanding of church in the twenty-first century.

'Awful,' he replied. 'I have had an awful day and wanted you to remind me again how great God's church really is.'

Apparently the aim of the conference had been to deconstruct the church, but it did nothing to rebuild any hope. The speaker had started the day by asking people to grade their disillusionment with the church by standing in different areas of the hall from the 'slightly disillusioned' to the 'very disillusioned'. My friend caused a storm when he asked where the area was for those who love the church and were not disillusioned, because they had no illusions about it in the first place. Apparently, there was no such area.

In stark contrast, King David felt the hope in Christian community when he wrote 'It made me glad to hear them say, "Let's go to the house of the Lord!"' (Psalm 122:1 CEV). So why is that so many of us are not glad when it comes to the church?

Look how far the church has moved from its roots. When the church had its first meeting on the Day of Pentecost, it was such a blast that people looking on thought the believers were drunk. I wonder if people looking on at many of our church meetings today would think we might have overdosed on Horlicks!

I have heard some commentators say that over time the initial flush of enthusiasm is bound to wane, like in any other organization. But I want to say that we are not like any other organization. We are a living, growing organism full of the dynamic power of the Holy Spirit. We are the Bride of Christ celebrating our imminent and intimate union with him. Jesus loved weddings. He began his ministry at one and told lots of stories about bridegrooms and wedding banquets. And the final book in the Bible says we will play out the last few days of human history at one humdinger of a wedding celebration that will see Jesus finally take us, his bride, to be his own. It seems we have lost sight of that hope – that spark of life. To put it bluntly, we have gone cold!

So how do we keep our passion hot for God's church despite the gloomy statistics of decline? How do we build churches that really work? The answer must be found in you and me. It's time to stop blaming others and take on our responsibility. Michael Green made this simple yet powerful observation: 'You do not need a church building or clergymen in order to grow the church. But you do need men and women who are passionate for Jesus and determined to make him known.'

When it comes to God's church on earth we need to move away from an attitude of resigned cynicism and start to fall in love with her again. A good friend of mine is a pastor in a growing church in the Midlands. He was asked to speak at a joint service with other churches in the area. Many of them were smaller and more traditional than his and struggling both with declining numbers and declining credibility. He had begun to prepare a talk about how the church is failing and how we need to pull our socks up or face extinction. But God spoke to him as he sat in his office preparing that day and reminded him how passionate he was about his bride and how proud he was about all that she was doing in his name. So my pastor friend wrote a new talk where he outlined all the great things the church was doing in the area like the drop-in centres, old-age clubs, youth-counselling services, homeless shelters, the list went on and on. He entitled his talk 'The church – alive and well'. The church was bringing hope to its community, which just needed reminding.

In his introduction to *Courageous Leadership*, Bill Hybels writes:

> What makes my heart beat fast is engaging with leaders in local churches, because I believe that the local church is the hope of the world. I believe it to the core of my being that local churches have the potential to be the most influential force on planet earth. If they 'get it,' and get on with it, churches can become the redemptive centers that Jesus intended them to be. Dynamic teaching, creative worship, deep community, effective evangelism, and joyful service will combine to . . . strengthen families, transform communities and change the world.

HOW TO MAKE IT WORK

If you feel as though you have fallen out of love with God's church and are feeling increasingly disillusioned with it, then below are three characteristics to cultivate. Three simple-to-remember words with some diagnostic questions that will motivate you to be part of a church that works by becoming passionate for Jesus and making him known. As you work through these ideas, don't lose sight of the aim – to fall in love with God's church and its mission all over again.

1. Authenticity

'When I first came to you . . . I didn't try to impress you with polished speeches and the latest philosophy. I deliberately kept it plain and simple' (1 Corinthians 2:1 MSG).

What Paul says here, and in many other parts of his letters, is that he always speaks with authenticity. 'I am not out to impress you but to be real about my feelings and my faith. You won't find any jargon or university degree lecturing from me. I will admit my weaknesses and model a life based on truth.'

When our small group started our first weekly meeting, coffee and pleasantries were done along with the obligatory ice-breaker. We went round the group talking about how we were doing in life. I was amazed as it went from person to person, everybody said they were flying high. No problems, no fears, no worries. Great spiritual growth, great faith and great trust abounded. I began to feel a little inadequate, as I began to make up a story that hid how I was really feeling inside. Then, just before it came round to me, it was Sonia's turn. She spoke with genuineness and authenticity about her temptations and failures. She confessed her spiritual dryness and her doubts. She finished with a tear in her eye and asked us to pray for her.

Our group changed that night. One after the other, people backtracked and told the truth about their lives. No pretence, no hiding.

Something very special was happening. God's people were learning to be real with each other. This authenticity became a hallmark of our group, and it became highly infectious in the wider church.

How's your level of authenticity? Ask yourself these three diagnostic questions:

- When was the last time you had an honest moment about your life with a friend?
- Who knows you – I mean, really knows you?
- How are you modelling authenticity in your church?

2. Grace

'Now God has us where he wants us, with all the time in this world and the next to shower grace and kindness upon us in Christ Jesus' (Ephesians 2:7 MSG).

We were so far from God once, you and me. We had let the world pollute us beyond belief. We were dead, with our backs turned to God and with hell in our sights. Then God's amazing grace gave us what we didn't deserve – a complete pardon from guilt, a new life and a home in heaven. Surely, since this is all our experience, the churches we are a part of must be a shining example of grace and forgiveness to other desperate strugglers in life. Surely it is the first place the sinner goes to for help. Well, you would think so, wouldn't you?

Philip Yancey recalled this amazing true story in his book *The Jesus I Never Knew*. It was told to him by a friend who works with homeless people in Chicago.

> A prostitute came to me in wretched straits, homeless, sick, unable to buy food for her two-year-old daughter. Through sobs and tears, she told me she had been renting out her daughter – two years old! – to men interested in kinky sex. She made more renting out her

daughter for an hour than she could earn on her own in a night. She had to do it, she said, to support her own drug habit. I could hardly bear hearing her sordid story. For one thing, it made me legally liable – I'm required to report cases of child abuse. I had no idea what to say to this woman. At last I asked if she had ever thought of going to a church for help. I will never forget the look of pure, naïve shock that crossed her face. 'Church!' she cried. 'Why would I ever go there? I was already feeling terrible about myself. They'd just make me feel worse.'

As a church leader I find that story heartbreaking. Yancey goes on to note how women much like this prostitute fled to Jesus for refuge when he walked the earth, yet those kinds of people are no longer welcomed among his followers today. We need to get back to our roots if we are ever going to build an inclusive church that works. And that could get a little messy and smelly at times.

For grace is what makes the church the hope for the world. We have what governments don't have. They can inject cash into a social crisis. They may be able to legislate to build affordable homes for the poor or create better hospitals for the sick. But where else can the world go to find grace but the church? It's our most important contribution to our society. Ask yourself these four *grace* diagnostic questions:

- How inclusive is your attitude to those far from God?
- When was the last time you felt out of your comfort zone as you came face-to-face with a person desperately in need of grace?
- How well informed are you about those who need grace in your local area?
- How well informed, involved and organized is your church or small group in bringing grace to those who are crying out for it?

3. Joy

'The next time you put on a dinner, don't just invite your friends and family and rich neighbours . . . invite some people who will never get invited out, the misfits from the wrong side of the tracks. You'll be – and experience – a blessing. They won't be able to return the favour, but the favour will be returned – oh, how it will be returned!' (Luke 14:13 MSG).

The order of these three characteristics of authenticity, grace and joy is no accident. Shoot first for authenticity in your relationships at church and show grace to a damaged and desperate world and the natural by-product will always be joy – unbridled, extreme, infectious joy. You just won't be able to keep the lid on it. The well-known, best-selling author and international speaker Tony Campolo writes in his book *The Kingdom of God Is a Party*:

> The church should gather together for worship after participating with God in winning victories for his kingdom in the world. If members of the congregation have led people to Christ or have championed the cause of justice, then when they get together they can give testimonies of these things, and in so doing get fellow Christians on a 'high'. After experiencing what God has done through them while scattered in the world, Christians find it easy to celebrate when they gather together for worship.

The church should be the starting point for people looking to experience the buzz of real joy. Not the movie theatre or the club or the sports field or the shopping mall. All these things can put a smile on your face but compared to experiencing the kind of long-lasting buzz God dispenses, they only scratch the surface. God is the happiest being in the universe and we are made in his image, so some of that happiness should be rubbing off on us. I just wonder if we might be looking for it in the wrong places. Endless worship services can seem increasingly shallow to many. But gather together to celebrate lost people getting found or hungry people getting fed or oppressed people finding justice, then you will see real joy capable of raising even the most traditional of church roofs!

The church. Just like at a football game, it's easy to sit on the touch-line and complain. It's a lot harder to stop being a spectator and start playing the game, but that's where the adventure is at its most sparkling. When Jesus said, 'I will build my church,' he wasn't talking about spires, sanctuaries and pulpits. He was talking people.

We get our word *church* from the Greek word *ekklesia*, which is best translated, 'the called out ones'. God's aim was, and still is, to call people whom he created to become his children. People who, with his power living in them, will go where he goes and do what he says; people who will love him, love his church and love its mission till he calls them home.

Are you really one of those people, full of authenticity, grace and unbridled joy? Or are you firmly rooted in the ranks of cynics who stand passively on the fringes? More than ever, I passionately believe that a church full of joy-infused, grace-giving, authentic Christ-followers really could become the hope of the world. A church so contagious – who knows where it might end up? Hold me back.

Part 5

GETTING NAKED AT WORK

16

THE GLUE THAT HOLDS OUR WAY OF LIFE TOGETHER

How to change your organization – whoever you are

NAKED LIFE

The author Max Lucado tells the amazing true story of Dr Evan Kane, who in 1921 was convinced that operations could be done with a local anaesthetic as opposed to the greater risks of administering a general one. He proved his point to the watching world when he removed his own appendix whilst under a local anaesthetic. The operation was a success, his recovery quick and a new medical discipline was born.

As you read this chapter, I am going to ask you to be equally as brave. I want you to do some inner self-surgery and ask yourself the probing question, Who am I really at work? Answering this as authentically as possible will affect the way you look at others and the way others look at you in the workplace. Let's start by thinking about your image in your workplace.

The world-renowned speaker and author John Maxwell writes, 'Image is what people think we are. Integrity is what we really are.'

He suggests that the more you concentrate on credibility and integrity rather than image, the more people will trust you to have a greater influence in their lives and therefore in their daily business. He comments that people at his conferences often say to him as they walk into the seminar room, 'I hope you can give me some insights into how I can change my business today, Mr Maxwell.' His response is always the same: 'My goal is to inspire you to change. Because if that happens, the organization you work for will also be changed.'

Business guru Peter Drucker in his book *Management Tasks, Responsibilities and Practices* cites a survey of 1,300 senior executives where 71 per cent put integrity at the top of a list of 16 performance enhancing traits for executive success.

So if we are going to make an impact at work, it will be less about sharp suits and snappy strap lines and more about credibility and integrity – matching our words to our lives. Let me show you what that looks like.

My friend Ian is a brilliant and successful self-employed architect. As we talked together at one of our many inspirational lunch meetings where we chat about business and life, he told me of an integrity dilemma that he faced recently. He was working on a large building project for a client with a local contracting firm of builders. To cut a long story short, a mistake was made and Ian was down to lose thousands of pounds in putting it right. He had the option of covering it up and no one would have been any the wiser, but he chose the integrity option and came clean. He decided to take the financial hit.

The contractor and client were astounded at his honesty. They commented to him that most architects would never have admitted fault. Rather, they would have covered it up or blamed someone else. The result was that, although this job cost Ian a great deal of money, the impressed contractors recommended him for many other highly lucrative jobs. He has got his money back and then some. He made an internal change, a decision to resist the lure of dishonesty, which upheld God's values in the workplace and gave him a chance to talk more of why he lives and works with this value held high. It also transformed his entire business right down the balance sheet.

As Ian commented,

> In my business I have discovered that integrity has to be about steering the right course in the face of a general drift towards lower standards and downright dishonesty. Defining what's right is tricky, but I guess it's the absolutes demonstrated by Jesus. Society tends to drift to the lowest common denominator, and today everything is seen as a shade of grey. In other words, there are no black-and-white situations. I believe integrity actually bucks that trend and simply states there is wrong and there is right. It is often not cool to be right about things. Using office stamps and stationery are common areas of theft. Being 'economic with the truth' is another, getting others to cover for you when you take a 'sickie' and the list goes on.

HOW TO MAKE IT WORK

How can we change the company we work for? What strategies can we adopt that will enable us to raise the bar on our integrity levels in the workplace? How can we concentrate on building credibility and not image? Let the surgery begin.

Strategy 1: Take the quick 'integrity vs image' assessment

'If we get this straight now, we won't have to be straightened out later on. Better to be confronted by the Master now than to face a fiery confrontation later' (1 Corinthians 11:31–32 MSG).

Answer true or false to these five questions to determine how you are doing on the image builder versus integrity builder stakes in the workplace.

1. No matter with whom I am working, I am the same person through and through.
2. No matter what others have achieved, I am the first to give authentic praise for their success.
3. No matter what the weight of opinion is, I will aim to make the right choices for everybody and not just for myself.
4. No matter how negative the atmosphere, I am known for having a positive attitude.
5. No matter how late others get to their workstations, I always arrive in good time.

Did you get mostly true or false answers? It doesn't take long to spot the image-driven people at work. They are the ones who promise much but deliver very little. Our aim must be to become people of integrity whose words match up to our lives and whose promises never disappoint.

Strategy 2: Make integrity your lifelong daily goal

'Are you still holding on to your integrity?' (Job 2:9).

Job's wife asks a good question of her husband because becoming a person of integrity is hard work. It goes against the grain – especially when life gets tough. Billy Graham said in a recent *Newsweek* article, 'Integrity is the glue that holds our way of life together. We must constantly strive to keep our integrity intact. When wealth is lost, nothing is lost; when health is lost, something is lost; but when character is lost, all is lost.'

Management guru Steven Covey wrote in his best-selling book *7 Habits of Highly Effective People*, 'Over the past 50 years leadership has focused on skills in management. In the future, leadership will focus on developing people of character, depth and integrity.'

The integrity factor doesn't come naturally in life. It will take daily effort to pursue it. You will face a variety of dilemmas, choices and decisions in any given day, many of which will be conflicting or confusing. Will you make a good or a bad choice? It's only your integrity levels that will determine which one prevails. Here are three ways to make daily choices that will enable you to keep your integrity muscles strong:

1. Make choices that are of high integrity even when you think no one is looking. The results will soon be seen as integrity becomes a way of life for you.
2. Make choices that will lead to other people putting their trust in you – and do it in the little things first. Things like using the company phone, your expenses, your time, your choice of humour and conversation topics. Get it right in these small things and people will know that your words in the next staff meeting can be trusted. It will show that you are a person who really means what you say.
3. Make choices that are thought out and not reactionary. Pause and pray before you decide. Take time to ask yourself and others what is the best decision to make before you make it.

Strategy 3: Use the hard times to grow in integrity

'Though [Jesus] was God's Son, he learned trusting-obedience by what he suffered, just as we do' (Hebrews 5:8 MSG).

It was the hard times that taught Jesus to grow in his character. A good testing point of your current integrity levels is when stress and pressure at work are at a peak – when deadlines are looming and tempers are on the edge. When your work life crashes into your inner life, you will soon discover what is genuinely inside you. Because it's at those times that it all comes pouring out. So when your work life is squeezed these days, do others you work with find a torrent of acceptance and forgiveness pouring out? Or is it more anger, bitterness and revenge that mark you out? Watch out for (and maybe even welcome) harsh criticism, ridiculous deadlines, unfair pay awards or promotions because your response to them could become a master class to others in how to live with integrity.

Integrity. Tell me that won't change your company! Think about it. Your company or organization needs you. It really does. It needs you to do the following:

- Be the kind of person who leads yourself well before you try to lead anyone else.
- Work hard for the benefit of the others within the organization and not just for yourself.
- Be close enough to those you work with to know their struggles and to be close enough to God to know how to help them.
- Be a person of great integrity in the micro stuff of daily living as well as the macro stuff of your company's next big project.

17

THE ONE ABOUT THE SHEEP AND THE PIGEON

How to make your work worthwhile every day

NAKED LIFE

The old story is told of a shepherd who was looking after his sheep on the side of a deserted road. Suddenly a brand new Porsche screeches to a halt. The driver, a young man dressed in an Armani suit, with Ray Bans, a Tag Heuer watch, Cerutti shoes, tailor-made mauve shirt, with a Boss tie, gets out and asks the shepherd, 'If I can guess how many sheep you have, can I keep one?'

The shepherd looks at the large flock of sheep and says, 'Okay.'

The young man connects his laptop to his mobile phone-fax, enters the NASA website, scans the field using his GPS, opens the database linked to 60 Excel tables filled with logarithms and pivot tables, then prints out a 150-page report on his high-tech mini printer. He studies the reports and says to the shepherd, 'You have 1586 sheep.'

The shepherd replies, 'That's correct. You can have the pick of my flock.' The young man packs away his equipment, looks at the flock and puts one into the boot of the Porsche. As he is about to leave, the shepherd says, 'If I can guess what your profession is will you return the animal to me?'

The young man thinks for a minute and says, 'Okay.'

The shepherd says, 'You are a Management Consultant.'

The young man replies, 'That is correct. How did you know?'

The shepherd replied, 'Simple. First, you came here without being invited. Second, you charge me a fee for something I already knew. Third, you don't understand anything about my business. Now . . . can I have my dog back please?'

Whatever your job – shepherd or management consultant, or anything else in between – you will no doubt find a level of frustration and disappointment that will lead you to ask the inevitable question, Why do I do what I do?

My first job when I left school at eighteen was with the supermarket chain Sainsbury's. I had enrolled on their three-year retail management programme in London and was more than a little nervous as I rode the early tube train on that first chilly winter's morning. I pulled out the best-wishes card from my jacket pocket that an old friend and mentor had given me the previous day. I still chuckle today when I recall his priceless office wisdom for me on my first day:

> Duncan, you will need to accept that some days you are the pigeon and some days you are the statue. You will also need to see the boss in a different perspective. So if she or he is getting you down then look at them through the prongs of a fork and imagine them in prison.

I left that job three years later to work in the marketing department of a ceramic tile company. I found that although the environment was different, many of the pressures were still the same. The people that I now spent every day with had different names, but they had very similar needs. I still felt like a pigeon some days and a statue others, and I still wished I could lock up the boss on more than one occasion.

Some days in those first few years of my working life I would ride the tube back home wondering what the point of going to work really was, wishing I was rich and didn't have to work and asking why I had to work in the first place. I guess I am not the only young person whose first few steps into the world of work had been faltering and whose fear and uncertainty about the future grew with every passing pay packet.

My dad had always repeated, 'I owe, I owe, it's off to work I go' as he walked out the door on Monday mornings. Maybe that was the reason I should go to work everyday. My friend's dad had decided to stay at home and not go to work at all. Maybe I could do the same and spend my days getting up late and slobbing out in front of the TV. If I could just find a sense of purpose in getting up early five mornings a week and spending the day with my nose to the grindstone then just maybe it would make the next forty-seven years of working life much more worthwhile.

As time went by I began to understand . . .

HOW TO MAKE IT WORK

There are so many myths about the whys and the whats and the hows of work. I want to take a moment to blow the lid off three of those myths and give you a fresh understanding of your motivation to do what you do every day. I want you to see your work as God sees it. And it might not be as you may think.

Myth 1: It's only work if I am paid to do it

'*And whatever you do, whether in word or deed, do it all in the name of the Lord Jesus*' (Colossians 3:17).

I have often heard it said, 'Boil work down to its basic ingredients and you come out with money. It has to be the only real motivation to work.' Try telling a hard-working college student spending her days in lectures and her evenings in libraries writing lengthy assignments that work is only what you get paid for. Try telling an older retired gentleman that keeping the home tidy, picking up the grandchildren from school and volunteering at the local community centre is not really work. Try telling the busy mum that running the household, being on call twenty-four hours for the children and serving in the church as a small group leader that her days don't count as work. They don't believe the myth that it's only work when you get paid for it. Whatever any of us do, whether paid or unpaid, is to be done to honour the name of Jesus.

I heard Tony Campolo talk recently of how frustrated his wife had become with the patronizing put down of well-meaning people who often asked, 'What is it you do, my dear?' Her well-fashioned answer makes the point brilliantly: 'I am socializing two Homo sapiens in the dominant values of the Judean Christian tradition so they become agents for the transformation of the social order into the kind of eschatological utopia God had in mind from the beginning of time . . . and what is it you do?'

Don't believe the myth that says work is only work if you are paid to do it. Whatever you do, do it in the name of Jesus.

Myth 2: I only work to pay the bills

'The Lord God took the man and put him in the Garden of Eden to work it and take care of it' (Genesis 2:15).

God, the worker, made us in his image and gave us the task of working the earth. So the way you work is a reflection of God's image in. you. That must be our motivation to work. It's the way we are made. So let's get the money thing straight. Money *is* an important issue in our work. Paul reminds Timothy that a worker is worth his wage (1 Timothy 5:18) and that not to provide for your family makes you worse than an unbeliever (1 Timothy 5:8). But money should never be the defining influence in our work. If we make earning money the *primary* focus of our daily toil, it will ultimately lead to a feeling of dissatisfaction because we will never earn enough to satisfy us. Human nature always says enough never will be enough. So we are to go about our work as if Jesus was the person we are working for and not simply so we can pay the bills. He is our motivator, our line manager, our supervisor or our board of directors. It is he we must work for every day and ultimately it is he who will reward us. And I get the feeling that his future prospects are far more certain and far more lavish than those of Wall Street or the Stock Exchange.

Myth 3: You can't bring God into the workplace

'And who knows but that you have come to a royal position for such a time as this?' (Esther 4:14).

Your work is your mission. After all, you probably spend about 65–70 per cent of your waking life there. Don't fall into the trap of sticking God into a Sunday box whilst leaving him out of the Monday-to-Friday arena of life. Just being at work will bring God's fragrance into people's lives. Can you imagine the sheer exhilaration of being used by God to bring his perspective into your business decisions and dilemmas or of seeing the lives change of those you work closely with or of being a part of shaping the culture of your entire company? Can you just image that? That's something worth getting up for on a Monday morning. Here are some simple prompts that will help you to begin to experience this daily thrill at your work. They are four very practical yet attainable ways for you to drag God into your everyday working life. You really can start this next Monday morning.

1. Don't go it alone

Make sure you are in a small group of like-minded people who promise to pray for each other and do life together. Keep in touch during the week on the phone or via email. Knowing someone is praying for you as you head into a tough appointment is a real strength giver. Finding a 'How did it go?' message on your voicemail on your return is a real encouragement.

2. Get a 'going to work' prayer habit

I have found a landmark near the office so as I drive in or out it prompts me to pray for the work that lays ahead and the people I will be working with.

3. Use your travel time to feed the mind

It's important not to switch off the news as you travel, but to let it provoke you to pray for the world around. But how about also making it a regular habit of listening to talks on tape that will feed your mind with God's Word?

4. Keep in touch

I often arrange to have lunch with people at work. An occasional visit or lunch or even a phone call during the day can prove to be a spiritual lifeline.

The workplace. In 1945 the Church of England realized that the workplace must become its key strategic priority if it was ever going to be relevant and effective in people's lives. It seems that many of us still need to wake up to this reality. Do you see your workplace as your God-given mission field?

We are convinced that England will never be converted until the laity use the opportunities daily afforded by their professions, crafts and occupations.

TOWARDS THE CONVERSION OF ENGLAND
(quoted in a recent publication by the London Institute
of Contemporary Christianity).

18

WHAT IF JESUS WAS YOUR BOSS?

How to hear God's applause at work

NAKED LIFE

How will you look back on your life? Will you reach old age with a sense of achievement or a sense of regret? Do you ever worry that the minister at your funeral will struggle to scrape together even a few adjectives to describe your life's work?

Leonard Wolf, an eminent British politician, felt this acutely. He looked back over his fifty plus years in the public eye at Westminster by concluding his autobiography with the following paragraph:

> Looking back at the age of 88 over the 57 years of my political work in England, knowing what I aimed at and the results, meditating on the history of Britain and the world since 1914, I see clearly that I achieved practically nothing. The world today and the history of the human anthill during the last 57 years would be exactly the same as it is if I had played Ping-Pong instead of sitting on committees and writing books and memoranda. I have therefore to make a rather ignominious confession to myself and to anyone who may read this book that I must have in a long life ground through between 150,000 and 200,000 hours of perfectly useless work.

How can we ensure that our work will never be described as 'perfectly useless'? Think about it this way. When you meet someone for the first time, the question asked more often than not is 'What do you do?' We are increasingly defined by what occupies our time every day. And if that comes with the tag MD, pilot or CEO, then giving an answer is enjoyable. But if it's a shop assistant, bus driver or housewife, then answering is not such a pleasurable experience. If we are not careful, the ambitions of our work can often end up as the emotional centre of our lives, the place we draw all our energy and significance from – and that's a dangerous place to be. As Gordon MacDonald once wrote in his *Leadership Journal*, 'First, you do not let work pass judgement on your self worth. Because when the job goes down the toilet, you don't want to be going down with it!'

Are we destined to spend our lives working simply to find significance, or is it possible to make our everyday activities really work for the best? I think it is. Just contrast Leonard Wolf's final lament on life with the apostle Paul's last words on planet earth:

'This is the only race worth running. I've run hard right to the finish, believed all the way. All that's left is the shouting – God's applause. Depend on it' (2 Timothy 4:7 MSG).

Below are three work strategies that will delight heaven itself. Begin to implement them today and then listen out for 'God's applause' as you catch the bus home next Friday evening.

HOW TO MAKE IT WORK

Even at a young age Jesus said he was about his father's business. He balanced listening to his father's instruction and then doing only what God wanted him to do with being highly strategic in his operations. (He told his disciples to start their evangelism business in Jerusalem and then move it in concentric circles out to the surrounding towns, counties and then eventually to go global.) So as you listen for the prod of God's spirit in your everyday working routines, use these three work strategies to build a strong foundation in your working life.

Strategy 1: Begin changing your attitude rather than changing your employment

'Now we look inside, and what we see is that anyone united with the Messiah gets a fresh start, is created new. The old life is gone; a new life burgeons! Look at it!' (2 Corinthians 5:17 MSG).

There is an apocryphal workplace parable about a new employee who, on her first day, asked the office manager what it was like to work in this office.

'Well, what was it like in your last office?' the wise manager asked.

'Terrible,' said the new employee. 'The work was boring and the people were mean to me.'

'I am afraid,' replied the manager, 'that you could well find the same true of this office.'

Later that day another new office junior started with the same question and was asked in return by the office manager what it was like at her old place.

'Oh, it was fantastic. The work really engaged me and the people were extremely friendly to work with.'

The wise office manager said, 'Then you will find this office just as wonderful as your last place.'

Your attitude *to* work will determine your actions *at* work. With the right attitude, work can actually become an enjoyable and fulfilling place to be. Maybe you can't do much about your menial tasks, your mean boss or your meagre pay, but you can do a lot about your attitude towards them.

I have discovered that my kids are at their worst when they are bored. They fight, squabble and complain. But if I am honest, I have also discovered that I am no different. I need to have an attitude that is alive during my daily routines. So if, as Paul says, you really are a new creation in your workplace, then you need to model what that newness might look like. No one wants to be around Negative Norman or Moaning Miranda or even Lazy Leslie. It just pulls them down too. But spend time working with someone with an attitude that is fully alive, then you find yourself coming alive too.

I have a friend who is a financial advisor. Before he became a Christian his sole aim in work was to make as much money as he could from his clients. Since he has made Jesus the leader of his life and his values, he has learnt to turn his job into a mission. It's now his aim to serve his clients' best interests, to go the extra mile with them, to care for them in a financial crisis and not to merely look out for his own financial gain. He has since become the most profitable advisor in the company because everybody wants him to manage their affairs. But more than that, this new God-given attitude to work has given him the one thing we all chase after – complete job satisfaction. He often hears the applause of heaven as he walks home at the end of a busy working week.

Strategy 2: Keep your excellence levels as high as possible

'Do your work willingly, as though you were serving the Lord himself, and not just your earthly master' (Colossians 3:23 CEV).

There is a wonderful story about the great Baptist preacher C.H. Spurgeon who asked the lady he employed to do his cleaning what was different about her work now she had become a Christian. 'I now sweep under the carpets,' she answered.

How would you describe your standards at work right now? Are you a just-do-the-bare-minimum type of worker or is good-enough-never-is your aim at work? Doing something really well gives any worker a sense of pride in the work and joy in its completion. It makes the working day and its tasks much more enjoyable.

I know it seems easier to continually raise the bar on excellence when you are a hotshot business guru earning millions from every deal, or a famous athlete breaking world records on the track, but how do we aim for the best when changing nappies or doing overtime in the complaints department? The key is to work as if Jesus was your supervisor. How would your daily tasks change? Think about it. If the boss asks you to nip out during your lunch break and pick up a client from the station, you may reluctantly tidy up the tapes in the car and clear out the kids' crisp packets off the back seat. But if it were Posh and Becks who were asking for a lift, you would give the car a complete valet inside and out! Look down your current task list and see how you might fulfil them as if it were God who was asking you to do it. Working with excellence in mind will bring you respect and give you great opportunities for telling others about the God who you live for. Then you will hear God's applause as you head for home.

Strategy 3: Earn loads so as to give loads away

'A simple life in the fear of God is better than a rich life with a ton of headaches' (Proverbs 15:16 MSG).

This was Paul's advice to thieves who once stole, but it must be one of the best reasons to get up and go to work each day – to serve others in need. Just doing it for money is not going to give you the ultimate job satisfaction you crave. Making money is no bad thing, but the real joy is in giving much of your wealth away to Christ and his mission.

I spoke recently to a lawyer who has made this principle his lifelong commitment to God. He is in his mid-forties and enjoying every minute of his working life as a high earner and an equally extravagant giver. Back in his university days, he realized the huge earning potential of his chosen career. So he made a vow to God that he would set himself a limit of what he needed to comfortably live on and then he would give the rest away – all of it! Now he lives in a nice suburban house with a smart car on the front drive, but he gives away far more than he keeps. His comment to me was:

> No matter how hard I try, I just can't stop earning money. The more I give away the more God seems to put back into my bank account ready for the next needy person or project. I have never had so much fun at work. I see the others fretting over the spiralling costs on their boats, holiday villas and third homes whilst I have the joy of seeing others thrive who were once at the point of desperation.

I am not sure that earning money to please ourselves will ever ultimately satisfy. Tony Campolo tells of how one rich businessman asked him if he thought buying a BMW was a sin. Campolo responded:

> I always have to ask myself what kind of car Jesus would buy if he was presently among us in the flesh. Would he spend $40,000 for a BMW? I doubt it. In the face of the desperate hunger and poverty that exists in the world today, I think Jesus would live more simply in order to use his resources to help those who are simply trying to live.

These three work strategies are designed to move us from being simply success driven to being driven by the desire to find authentic significance in our working lives. A desire to grow our attitudes right, raise our standards high and serve others well. Shhh . . . What's that distant noise? It can't be . . . I think I can just hear the applause – God's applause. Can you hear it yet?

19

THE MAN WITH THE DATSUN CHERRY

How to be a diligent leader

REAL LIFE

I read with great interest a recent landmark *Wall Street Journal* article entitled 'World Leadership Crisis'. The subject got me thinking deeply as most leadership subjects do. Then that very same day I heard Bill Hybels highlight the same issues I had found in the article during a talk he gave at a international leadership conference I was attending. He said:

> People don't want to be managed; they long to be led. Who ever heard of a world manager? World leader, yes; educational leader, political leader, religious leader, community leader, business leader – they all lead. They don't manage. Our twenty-first century world needs less management and more leadership.

I know from experience that leadership is the key for developing the potential of any organization, be it a multi-national business or a local church. I also know that management is of vital importance, but management alone will only lead to maintenance. What's the difference between the two? Hybels sums it up well by saying,

'Managers ensure that people are doing their daily routines, but leaders determine whether those routines are worth doing at all.'

In my case, I found it difficult to own my leadership responsibilities. I couldn't decide if I was a leader or still an emerging leader. What should a leader look like when she or he has emerged? What really is a leader anyway?

Below is the kind of confusing diary entry that indicates my dilemma of a few years ago.

Duncan's Diary

I am thirty years old and often considered as a leader waiting to emerge. I am one of the youngest in the room at most Christian leadership gatherings I attend. My leadership uniform is fashioned more from the Next casual wear department than the Marks and Sparks formal range – more jeans and T-shirts than slacks and Pringle diamond sweaters. I guess that makes me look more emerging than emerged. In fact, in these circles I am looking forward to the day when I will emerge. I'll wake up that sunny morning, rest my tea cup on my Christian Puzzler, re-tune to Terry on the breakfast show, slip out of my cocoon and fly away on the wings of an emerged leader. But when will that be? When I'm forty? Fifty? Or is it nothing to do with age but fashion and language and networks of relationships. Speak at Spring Harvest and you're still emerging but get on the speaking team at Keswick and the next step is to apply for the Trinity.

Or should it have read more like this?

Duncan's Diary

I am thirty years old and considered a well-established leader who ought to let go of the reigns for a younger generation chomping at the bit. My 'three child' status and modest family saloon mean I must be getting on a bit. My leadership jeans aren't baggy enough and my T-shirt not labelled correctly – more Next sale than Tommy

Hilfigger. I guess that makes me look more emerged than emerging. I wake up in the morning, rest my herbal tea on my Alan Titchmarsh gardening book, tune into Radio Five, slip out of my warm BHS floral duvet and splutter through the day on the wings of a leader with increasing amounts of pressure and responsibility. When did I emerge? Twenty-five, thirty? Or was it speaking at Spring Harvest where I was considered over the hill or speaking at Soul Survivor where the next step was my application to present Top of the Pops!

Both those opening paragraphs were true for me and often at the same time. I was a leader who was both emerged and emerging. Maybe it's my short hair cut, but I still stumble over these same feelings today. At a recent Evangelical Alliance gathering of key leaders, I had just finished a conversation with one man about his desire to use my book *Breakfast with God* as a devotional tool for new Christians in his church, when a well-suited gentleman who presumed me to be the venue caretaker approached me. He asked if I would be kind enough to pop out and check on his blue Datsun Cherry during the session as it was on a yellow line. It seemed easier to nod in agreement than explain. (I'm not sure he was best pleased with the parking ticket he no doubt got as he left later that day. Sorry!)

So, if you and I are ever going to reach our full leadership potential, we need to come to grips with what leadership is and how we can use it as diligently as the Bible commands that we should (Romans 12:8).

Leadership isn't just about influence. One longing look from my six-month-old son, Joe, may influence me to stay and play a little longer, but that doesn't make him a candidate for the church elders.

So what *is* leadership about? Max DePree, in his brilliant little book *The Art of Leadership*, gives three clear pointers: 'The first responsibility of any leader is to define reality. The last is to say thank you and in between the leader is a servant.'

HOW TO MAKE IT WORK

So let me take my leadership responsibilities seriously and serve you by defining three 'leadership realities' that may well help you with your leadership, be it emerged or emerging, be you a senior or a junior. These are three attainable steps that will enable you to lead diligently whether you are a Sunday school leader or the CEO of a large organization.

Leadership reality #1

The key to being an effective leader is growing more effective leaders. Grow strong leaders and you'll grow a strong organization. Grow weak leaders and the opposite is true. We need to be aware of the specific gifts of those we lead and ensure that their roles match them. An effective leader is one who will develop other leaders and not let that task drift to the bottom of the agenda. In his book *Spirituality and Leadership*, Alan Nelson comments:

> An effective leader is a matchmaker who marries people and roles. There are no wrong people, just wrong positions. The leader's job is to help people succeed. The best chance of this is by placing them in positions that unleash their talents.

So do a gift check. Start with yourself and ask, Do my strengths still match my role? Am I still passionate about what I am doing every day? Then ask, Am I maximizing the potential of future generations of leaders?

Leadership reality #2

The key to being an effective leader is continually communicating a clear vision. 'Where there is no vision, the people perish' (Proverbs 29:18 KJV).

Many years ago I was the youngest and newest staff member of a church. Things didn't go well and I was asked at a particularly painful elders' meeting to resign because I was leading the church away from its vision. I inquired as to what that vision was. Unfortunately none of the ten-man eldership team could answer me. Eventually someone pulled from a filing cabinet a booklet entitled 'Our Church Vision'. It contained a very long five-year vision statement that had been allowed to drift past the conscience of most people including the leaders. It had also run out a year previously and no one had known. In short the church was visionless. No wonder I struggled from the start and no wonder other leaders struggled with me. No church or organization should ever depend on a new leader to bring vision. It needs to decide on its purpose and then appoint staff around the dream. Clear roles and expectations then make for a powerful pulling together of gifts towards a common goal.

Before staff are hired, any church or organization needs a clear and specific purpose. A memorable and attainable goal that gives energy and creates focus. For Disney it's to make people happy. For Honda it's to beat General Motors. What is it for your organization and for your church? If a company that sells entertainment or cars needs a statement of intent, how much more does God's bride need one? That vision needs to be lived out by leaders and cast again and again until people's feet are lined up behind it.

So do a vision check. Does your church or organization or department have a clear and simple vision statement to aim for? Could they repeat it back if asked? Do you measure its success? Are your leaders working together to achieve it?

Leadership reality #3

The key to being an effective leader is having fun while you do it. 'What has happened to all your joy?' (Galatians 4:15).

Max DePree comments that 'joy is an essential ingredient of leadership and leaders are obligated to provide it.' Walk into any room of people and you'll hit it off with some and struggle with others. It is the chemistry of human nature. So when deciding who will be on our teams, who will surround us as we serve, we need to find people of great character and great ability but also people who we have affinity with. We are going to spend long periods of time together, so we have to be able to enjoy it enough to come back to work and do it all again the following day.

So do a 'joy level' check. Joy is highly contagious so ask yourself this question: Is my working environment mainly a fun place to be? Are my close leadership relationships full of joy or full of sadness and struggle? Am I surrounding myself with leaders who spark me and feed into me, or are they a constant drain?

I've now done two out of the three of Max DePree's leadership responsibilities that I quoted at the top of this chapter. Firstly, I have tried to *serve* you as best I can with these leadership ideas and then I have been as *real* as possible about leadership life. And so as Max says, here's my last leadership responsibility . . . *thanks*.

Thanks for taking the time to sharpen your skills by reading this chapter!

Part 6

GETTING NAKED WITH YOUR MONEY

20

THE WORLD
IS NOT ENOUGH
How to win the materialism battle

NAKED LIFE

A true-to-life classic tale . . .

A very rich and successful business executive was holidaying on an exclusive Greek island. As he walked along the beautiful quayside one afternoon, he came across a wizened-faced fisherman sleeping in the sun alongside his old fishing boat. He stopped, looked at him quizzically and walked on. The following afternoon the executive takes the same stroll in the sun and sees the fisherman once more, asleep in the sun beside his boat. As the businessman walks past again on the third day he stops by the man, wakes him and asks, 'Excuse me for asking, but why are you not out fishing?'

'I went out fishing this morning,' the old man replies. 'This afternoon I sleep.'

'But why don't you fish in the afternoon as well?' the executive asks.

'Tell me why I would want to do that?'

'Well, then you could double your catch of fish. Which will in turn double your profits. Then you could buy a bigger, smarter and newer boat. In time you could expand your business and even take on some staff to run the boat for you.'

'And then what?' the sceptical fisherman asks.

'Then you could enjoy life the way you have always wanted to enjoy it,' concludes the executive in triumph.

'And what,' asks the fisherman before closing his eyes to sleep again, 'do you think I am doing right now?'

Honestly, when is enough, enough? No really? When are we going to stop making the acquisition of things our life's ambition? 'Whoever loves money never has money enough; whoever loves wealth is never satisfied with his income' (Ecclesiastes 5:10).

If we make acquiring more our primary focus, we will end up more and more dissatisfied with life because enough never is. John D. Rockefeller, once the richest man in the world, was asked how much money you need in life to make you really happy. His answer was extremely insightful: 'Just a little bit more.' It seems so many of us have bought into the desire of every advertising executive whose aim is that we see life's little luxuries as can't-do-without necessities. In his book *Carpe Diem*, Tony Campolo talks about the advertising industry's ever more sophisticated appeal to those of us whose basic needs have already been satiated:

> Hamburgers are sold by appealing to our sense of losing out on life: 'you deserve a break today . . . at McDonalds.' In reality all you get for your money is some ground meat. 'Buick is something you can believe in!' Here you thought Buick was an automobile, and the ad makers tell you it's a religious conviction. Then there is the most famous ad of all time. In it we are shown people from all the nations of the world, dressed in their native costumes . . . holding hands and singing in unison, 'I'd like to teach the world to sing in perfect harmony . . .' And what is it that brings perfect harmony to broken humanity? It's Coca-Cola. And if there's any doubt about

the validity of the claim, a strong authoritative voice assures us, 'it's the real thing.'

Fashion now demands a new wardrobe every season and it must be the latest labels. Homes, we are told, deserve the latest gadgets designed to make our lives just that little bit easier. Even your hair care products are worth the extra L'Oreal price tag and why ... *because you're worth it!* It seems we still believe the old adage that the grass is always greener on the other side of the fence. How often have you ordered a dessert after a posh meal and when you compare it with the person's next to you, it's always the wrong choice?

If it is the aim of a generation to make as much money as they are spending, how do we ensure that we don't get sucked in? How do we avoid the twenty-first century trap that demands you work as hard as you can to earn as much money as you are able so as you can buy more things you can't really afford to impress people you don't really like anyway? How do we survive the cancer of consumerism and march away from the misery of materialism?

HOW TO MAKE IT WORK

'Do not wear yourself out to get rich; have the wisdom to show restraint' (Proverbs 23:4).

Below are three keywords that will help you do just that. Three simple-to-remember signposts that will help you get some clear direction as you navigate the choppy waters of managing your money wisely. Follow them closely and you could be well on the way to discovering more freedom financially.

Keyword 1: Contentment

'Actually, I don't have a sense of needing anything personally. I've learned by now to be quite content whatever my circumstances. I'm just

as happy with little as with much, with much as with little. I've found the
recipe for being happy whether full or hungry, hands full or hands empty'
(Philippians 4:11–12 MSG).

My friend, the British evangelist J. John, has often quoted this now famous little ditty:

> Money can buy medicine, but not health
>
> Money can buy a house, but not a home
>
> Money can buy companionship, but not friends
>
> Money can buy entertainment, but not happiness
>
> Money can buy food, but not an appetite
>
> Money can buy a bed, but not sleep
>
> Money can buy a good life, but not eternal life.

So if money can buy you Hilton-style comfort but can't buy you a linen cupboard of contentment, why do we still worship it so much? The awesome advice of G.K. Chesterton rings loud in my mind: 'There are two ways to get enough. One is to accumulate more and more and the other is to desire less.'

As the old saying goes, there is a big difference between making a living and having a life. So learn to be content with your circumstances. Be grateful for what you already have. List them out – I bet it's a longer list than you first thought. You may never have eaten at a banquet table, but you probably had a meal today. You may never have lived in a palace, but you probably had shelter last night. You may not have a mobile phone full of 'A' list celebs to call, but you probably have at least one person in your life who treats you like a VIP now and again. You are richer than you think. You can find contentment when you wake up to the fact that your life doesn't consist of how many things you have accumulated over the years but in something that can never be taken away – God's single-minded passion for you, his precious child.

Keyword 2: Perspective

'It's better to obey the LORD and have only a little, than to be very rich and terribly confused' (Proverbs 15:16 CEV).

We come into this world with nothing and we leave the same way.

Max Lucado writes about a 1923 'economic summit' at which nine of America's richest and most powerful businessmen and politicians gathered. Fabulously rich, incredibly powerful and internationally influential, these men lived lives that most people only dreamt of. But where are they now?

> Charles Schwann, a steel-company chief, died bankrupt, his last five years spent as a chronic depressive with weekly visits to the psychiatrist. Howard Hobson, an oil magnate, died insane in a mental asylum. The head of a corporate monopoly committed suicide as did the President of the International Bank of Settlements. Jesse Livermore, famous top Wall Street broker, also killed himself. Samuel Insell (head of a utility company), Richard Whitney (head of the New York Stock Exchange) and Arther Cruton (the great wheat speculator) all got into trouble with the law. Insell and Cruton died as fugitives abroad, on the run from the police; Whitney spent a lengthy term in Sing Sing prison and died bankrupt. Finally, Albert Fulwell, the Presidential Cabinet member, was pardoned from prison so that he could die at home, eaten up with disease.

Satisfaction never really came in life for those richest of men because as Jesus once told his followers, 'A man's life does not consist in the abundance of his possessions' (Luke 12:15).

Change your perspective on wealth and the acquisition of it. Ask yourself if your priorities are the right way up these days. Think about what drives and motivates you most in life? Then ask yourself the biggy: Where's your heart? Find the answer to that and you will find where your treasure really is.

Keyword 3: Generous

'Command them to do good, to be rich in good deeds, and to be generous and willing to share' (1 Timothy 6:18).

If I were writing the Obvious Version of the Bible, I would translate this verse like this:

> Here are six surefire ways to please God and find contentment –
> give, give, give, give, give . . . and when you have done all that, give
> some more . . . oh and by the way . . . that's not a suggestion – it's a
> command!

I know this might sound shocking in today's must-have-more culture, but giving to others is the best antidote I know to breaking a materialistic mindset. There is so much joy in giving. You could buy a new CD each month and keep up with the latest music trends, or you could spend that same amount of money on sponsoring a child with Compassion, giving them an education, health and a hope for the future. You could upgrade your car, your home or your wardrobe, or you could help your church make significant gains in seeing people who are far away from faith come close. You could take out a loan for another holiday this year that will top up your tan for a few weeks, or you could make an investment in somebody who needs it that will change their life forever.

Think about it: Where's the biggest pay-off going to come for you – in getting more or in giving more? We are made in the image of God – the greatest and most joyful giver ever. He gladly bankrupt heaven so you could have life. There is something in all of us that calls us to do the same. Can you feel it? Ask yourself these three self-diagnostic questions to find out how you are doing with giving:

1. Does my regular giving to God and those in need match up
   well in proportion to my regular income?

2. Do I ask God often about how he wants me to give my time and money?
3. If my friends knew how much I gave, would it be a challenge or a letdown to them?

Beware. Many preachers and authors throw in a 'be sensible' caveat at this point. 'Don't give beyond your means.' Not me. Sorry. It's just that I can't believe outrageous generosity to God and his people will ever damage you. The hymn writer John Wesley once said, 'Christians should work as hard as they can to make as much money as they can so as they can give away as much as they can.'

Mastering materialism. Ask yourself this: Have you become a material giant and a spiritual midget? Be honest with yourself. Have you gotten a hold of the money issue in your life or has money gotten a hold of you? Enough is enough when you learn to be content with what you have and not constantly chasing after just a little bit more and a little bit more and a little bit more and . . .

21

MY RESIGNATION
How to stay out of debt

NAKED LIFE

I am hereby officially tendering my resignation as an adult. I have decided I would like to accept the responsibilities of an eight year old again. I want to go to McDonald's and think it's a four-star restaurant. I want to sail sticks across a fresh puddle and make ripples with rocks. I want to think M&M's are better than money because you can eat them. I want to lie under a big oak tree and run a lemonade stand with my friends on a hot summer's day. I want to return to a time when life was simple. When all you knew were colours, multiplication tables and nursery rhymes, but that didn't bother you because you didn't know what you didn't know and you didn't care. All you knew was to be happy because you were blissfully unaware of all the things that should make you worried or upset.

I want to think the world is fair. That everybody is honest and good. I want to believe that everything is possible. I want to be oblivious to the complexity of life and be overly excited by the little things again. I don't want my day to consist of computer crashes, mountains of paperwork, depressing news and how to survive more days in the month than there is money in the bank.

So here's my chequebook and my car keys, my credit card bills and my financial statements. I am officially resigning from adulthood, and if you want to discuss this further, you are going to have to catch me first – because tag, you're it!

How many times have you felt like that recently? Is the pressure of balancing the books each month getting too much to bear? Do you want to leave your mounting credit card bills and your car keys with someone else and then run off into the woods to hide?

A shocking survey recently released by the Citizen's Advice Bureau says their debt advisers across the UK have reported a 47 per cent increase in the number of new consumer credit debt problems over the past five years. And they argue that the numbers nationally in debt have gathered pace. In a survey of 8,000 debt case studies, CAB found that the average amount owed was £10,700 – roughly 14 times their average monthly income of £800.

What does that actually look like in a person? BBC News Online talked recently to one such young man who will be paying off his credit card debts for six years. He is typical of many young people who enjoy going out with friends, buying nice clothes and splashing out on a foreign holiday or two each year. He is also one of a growing number of twenty- and thirty-somethings who have fallen prey to the ease of consumer credit – in the form of cards and loans – only to find their finances spiralling out of control.

> I got my first credit card in 1996 after leaving school and it really just went from there. Once I'd spent my pay packet for the month I'd just take out £50 here and there on my card, not thinking it would make much difference. It was just all so easy. Credit card leaflets would just fall through the door. I was never really questioned when I applied for credit, and never had to lie about other money I owed. And the more I owed, the more my credit limit was raised without me even asking.

Debt is a really complex subject and I don't profess to be anywhere near expert on the subject. In fact, if you are overwhelmed

with debt right now, I would encourage you to contact the experts.
You could try Credit Action (their freephone number is 0800
591084) or maybe your local Citizen's Advice Bureau. People get into
debt for many reasons, from struggling students and single parents,
to people unable to work through redundancy or illness. But figures
show that the majority of people in debt are there because of bad
spending habits and poor money management. It's in this area that I
want to try and help you get it right.

HOW TO MAKE IT WORK

So how do we grow up financially and avoid the ever-growing debt
trap? This is a very important one to crack if we are going to make life
work. Mainly because the way you deal with your financial life will
have a direct impact on the quality of your spiritual life. Your money
management has a greater bearing on the shape of your inner life
than you realize. You will do well to find 600 verses on prayer in the
Bible, but look up "money" and you find over 2,300. Jesus talked
about it more than he talked about heaven and hell. So below is a
three-point debt avoidance plan that will prove a wise long-term
investment, with an excellent return for your soul.

Do an 'attitudes and actions' reality check

'Wake up! You have only a little strength left, and it is almost gone'
(Revelation 3:2 CEV).

Be brutally honest with yourself about two things.

1. What's your attitude towards money?

Your financial *actions* will be spoilt if your financial *attitude* is
wrong. What are the signs of a financial attitude that's on the slide?
Maybe it's things like bills often going unpaid, impulse buying regard-
less of cost, working long hours to afford your chosen lifestyle, a con-

stant comparison of others that leads to greed or a how-can-I-get-rich-quick mentality in life.

2. What's your current financial situation?

Many of us have a distorted picture of the state of our own finances. We have no real idea of what money is going in and coming out. The ATM just keeps coughing up when we punch in the right sequence of numbers. Then suddenly we are faced with a mountain of unpaid bills and we ask ourselves how we got to this point. Getting an accurate picture of your current financial situation will enable you to reduce your spending.

Do a comprehensive budget and stick to it

'It takes careful planning for things to go right' (*Proverbs* 15:22 CEV).

The story is told of a dinner party where several young couples were discussing the difficulties in sticking to a budget. 'I really don't want a lot of money,' said one. 'I just wish we could afford to live the way we are living now!' I have friends who say they know that they should be budgeting but are afraid at what a budget may show up and that it may curtail their chosen lifestyle. The opposite is in fact true. The only way to find genuine financial freedom and contentment is in being real about where you are at financially, doing a budget and sticking to it. I would much prefer to be sitting on a sofa I have saved for watching the game on a TV I have paid for, than having a nagging worry inside wondering what I will do next month, and the 36 months after that, to meet the payments.

So how do I prepare a simple budget? Well, believe it or not, you don't need a degree in accountancy to do it. Budgeting is more straight forward than you think and can be very rewarding. Just think, for the first time you could really be in control of your money rather than the other way round. Start by adding up all your income streams (including overtime, family tax credits, savings, etc.). Next add up all your outgoings. You'll need to do this in three sections. First the big stuff (giving, mortgage payments, utility bills, council tax, car tax, etc.). Next, the everyday stuff (food, meals out, parking, kids' pocket money, etc.). Finally the odd stuff (birthdays, Christmas, holidays, home repairs, etc).

You could well find that your outgoings are bigger than your income. Breath a sigh of relief that you have found this out before it gets too serious. You have two choices now: Increase your income or reduce your outgoing. It may be tough to increase what comes in, but you will be able to reduce what you spend. It will take some difficult decisions like cancelling your sky package or your mobile phone contract or your health club subscription, but the enormous freedom it will give you is worth the sacrifice. (Doing those three things alone could save you about £150 a month – that's £1,800 a year!) For some it may take some big decisions to get back on track like selling a car or even downsizing a home.

Always take a wise friend shopping with you

'If you keep a cool head, you'll avoid rash bargains' (Proverbs 11:15 MSG).

One recent CAB survey said that credit card users spend 34 per cent more than those who don't. So when the day comes that you haven't got the money to pay a credit card bill, get out the scissors and cut your card into lots of little pieces! If you have any desire to manage your money well and keep out of debt, then you will have to reign in your impulse spending. That's why I suggest you think about taking a friend with you to the shopping mall. Someone who won't say, 'Go on, get it – you deserve it' but who will give you wise counsel and help you keep a cool head. Learn to be happy with what you already have and budget for what you need.

Check regularly on how you are doing

Ask yourself these six financial 'honesty' questions on a monthly basis. They are aimed at checking your heart and your attitude when it comes to money. They will help you avoid the debt trap and keep you on the right track.

1. Is my standard of living set right, or am I trying to live beyond my means?
2. Am I managing to save, even if it is a small amount each month?
3. Am I managing to give regularly to my local church and to those in need?
4. Am I making good spending choices based on my needs rather than my wants?
5. Am I winning the battle over the advertisers?
6. What would I really do if I were given a £50,000 windfall?

Beating debt. Get it all in perspective. 'The earth and everything on it belong to the Lord' (Psalm 24:1 CEV) – he owns the lot. 'Simply put, if you're not willing to take what is dearest to you . . . and kiss it goodbye, you can't be my disciple' (Luke 14:33 MSG).

He wants you to let go of everything you have but him. You see, he is not against you having things, but he doesn't want things to have you. So tell me again, who owns your house, your car, your wardrobe, your schedule, your career plan, your loved ones, your time off? You can do this. Be ruthless in importing biblical principles into finances, and you will see your whole life change.

22

STAYING OUT
OF THE STORMS

How to stay afloat financially

NAKED LIFE

The sweet shop. My final frontier. This was my fifteen-minute mission to boldly go where no eight year old had been allowed to go before.

It was the days of Captain Kirk's *Enterprise* and, along with my best mate from school, I had set off on a galactic adventure dressed as my space-faring hero. It was a dangerous mission across the barren land of the local wreck towards the new life and new civilizations to be found in the outer reaches of the corner shop. I had convinced Starfleet Command (that would be Mum and Dad) that I was now sufficiently experienced to go for my space sweets on my own. I knew that many dangers lay ahead and that anything could happen. I also knew that if I failed this mission and were not back in the allotted time, my little space bottom would have had a visit from the evil Mr Smack. I packed everything I needed in my space utility belt, including my phaser (bought from Woolworths for £2.99 and set on kill) and my communicator (Mum's old compact). 'Warp factor 6,' I shouted to Mr Sulu (that would be my friend George who was spending the day at my house) as we headed at top speed out of the front door and across the street.

Our pace had slowed as we walked through the wreck, picking off enemy trees as we went. We eventually orbited the high street and sent down a landing party to collect our samples from the sweet shop. We presented our bags of goodies to Alan the alien behind the counter. (My fertile imagination had turned his interesting facial acne into that of a vicious Klingon!) Suddenly calamity struck. I had forgotten to bring something to pay with. As I searched my utility belt for my pocket money, I realized that I may well have been prepared for shooting any aliens with my phaser, but I was completely unprepared to pay for my sweets. As the space tears of sadness and embarrassment trickled down my cheeks, I wished my communicator compact really could have got through to my mother ship. I just wanted to be beamed right out of there as quick as possible.

You may think that not being able to pay for your sweets is no big deal compared to your present financial struggles. Maybe for you it's a mortgage payment or a credit card bill that has drawn tears down your face recently. Does your financial storm leave you wishing you could just flick open your communicator and scream 'Beam me up, Scotty'? If only solving life's problems were really that easy, eh?

HOW TO MAKE IT WORK

It could be that you are going through a really rough financial storm right now and are feeling totally unprepared. It may well be tough, but just maybe this storm will do you good and teach you a life lesson you will never forget. Here are three steps you can begin to take today that will help keep you afloat financially both now and for the long term.

Step 1: Throw stuff overboard that you just can't afford

'Fearing for their lives, the desperate sailors . . . threw the cargo over-board to lighten the ship' (Jonah 1:5 NLT).

When the 'desperate sailors' sharing Jonah's ship thought it was going down, they threw whatever they didn't need into the sea to balance the ship and keep it afloat. Your financial storms may well need those same desperate measures to keep you from going down.

For my thirtieth birthday my wife saved up and bought me a trip of a lifetime – an hour-long flight over the English countryside in a hot air balloon. Twelve ballooning novices climbed into the basket and up we went, waving to family and friends as we ascended into the early evening sky. Gerry, the young, longhaired, Australian captain, started off the basket banter as we all confessed our various professions. They ranged from a concert pianist, an engineer, a housewife, an advertising executive to me – a church leader.

The flight was going extremely well until a freak strong wind came up heralding a storm that began pushing us way off course. At first it was an adventure, but then it all got a bit serious and we began to wobble and sway around in the rapidly dampening sky. Desperate measures were needed. Gerry announced we needed to make an emergency landing. Fearing for his life, the nervous concert pianist turned and asked me to do something. He meant pray, but for a laugh I suggested a baptism or a collection for the missionary fund. Gerry said we needed to lighten the load to get us down in one piece. He went about throwing all the sandbags over the edge and then moved onto to any extra luggage we had. (My denim jacket is still nestling in a tree somewhere near Worcester.) As we got lower to the ground, more stuff went over the edge, but it meant that after a few bumps we eventually landed safely.

You get the picture, don't you? If you are going to get a safe landing in the midst of your financial storm, you are going to need to lighten the load. For some it may mean dropping the mortgage by moving to a smaller house. For others it may mean driving a cheaper car, eating out less or reducing your wardrobe. It could be that you will need to sell furniture, TVs or computer games to raise cash, but you need to throw overboard whatever is necessary to save you from going down. I visited a couple recently who were tens of thousands of pounds in debt and yet were still spending a staggering £1,000 more a month than they were earning. They needed to throw overboard their mobile phones, internet packages, cars and clothes in order to stop the rot. They are also considering downsizing their home.

What cargo do you need to throw out in order to keep you stable?

Step 2: Learn from the ant and start a savings account

(Quick tip: Remember the big guy from the 1980s TV show *The A Team*? If you do, then read this verse out loud in a Mr T voice.)

'You lazy fool, look at an ant. Watch it closely; let it teach you a thing or two. Nobody has to tell it what to do. All summer it stores up food . . . so how long are you going to laze around doing nothing? . . . You can look forward to a dirt-poor life, poverty your permanent houseguest!' (Proverbs 6:6–11 MSG).

Ants get it. They store up food when the sun shines so as they can still eat when the winter storm hits. So why can't we get it? I read an article recently on consumerism reporting that 40 years ago the average American saved over 7 per cent of disposable income compared to today's average saving of just 0.2 per cent. According to research, the average person in the UK has no savings at all. This means that most of us have no reserves to draw on when a financial storm comes our way. So make it your aim to save regularly even if it is just a small amount each month. Once you have given the first part of your income to God each month, make sure it is your next task to put by an amount from your budget that will be available to you in the future when you most need it. Some people have it redirected from source straight into a savings account so they are not tempted to touch it.

Wise old Solomon says, 'Steady plodding brings prosperity' (Proverbs 21:5 TLB).

So set yourself some saving goals. Goals for the shorter term like replacing cars, family holidays or home improvements. And goals for the longer term like your children's education and your retirement. Being prepared in this way will ensure that you will be much less likely to go under when a financial storm blows your way.

Step 3: Play the savings game and teach the kids to do the same

'You must teach [these commandments] to your children and talk about them when you are at home or out for a walk' (Deuteronomy 6:7 TLB).

What are you planning on leaving your kids? The greatest gift you can give them is the example of your everyday life lived with Jesus as your leader. But hot on the heels of that is the gift of wise money management. Teach them good financial practises and model it in your own life. Then when they hit college age and every credit card company under the sun is offering them their services, they will be well equipped to say no and stay out of the storm.

When our boys started school, we decided to give them pocket money and used this to teach them the value of budgeting. Matthew's last words to me this morning as he left for school were, 'Dad, can you bring my save pot to school when you pick me up. I've got enough to buy some more action figure cards' (the latest school yard craze). Each of our lads has three pots: one marked GIVE, one SAVE and one SPEND. We teach them that when Mum and Dad get any money the first thing we do is to *give* a percentage to God and to those in need, then we *save* some for holidays, car repairs, clothes, etc. and the rest we use to *spend* on everyday stuff like food and of course some sweeties! We give them their pocket money in small coins and teach them to follow our model. It's a tough lesson for them to learn, but you should see the joy on their faces when they finally save enough to buy themselves a toy or a gift for someone else. I am more convinced than ever that if we teach these values to our children, they will grow up to weather the inevitable financial storms by becoming habitual savers rather than addicted credit junkies.

Life's financial storms. Sometimes they can be desperate and require desperate measures to get out of them. But surely the best thing is not to get in them in the first place.

This all became real to us as a family last week. We are currently looking for a new home in Suffolk. We set ourselves a budget that meant we could afford the monthly mortgage payments without killing ourselves. But then we came across *that* house. It was beautiful, but it was £25,000 over our budget. We did all we could to get to the asking price and were so close to agreeing a deal when Debbie did the sums. It turns out that if we had bought that house, we would have had to empty all our savings and would not be able to save any more in the future. After all the bills, it would have left us with a mere £44 a month disposable income. Boy am I glad we didn't buy that house. We would have gone under at the slightest hint of a storm!

Part 7

GETTING NAKED FOR THE FUTURE

23

A TIME CAPSULE
FOR MY BOYS

How to press values into their futures

NAKED LIFE

> Gather ye rosebuds while ye may
> Old time is still a flying,
> And that same flower that smiles today,
> Tomorrow will be dying

That was a line of a Robert Herrick poem quoted in my all-time favourite movie, *Dead Poets Society*, starring my all-time favourite actor, Robin Williams. And the scene that always draws the most emotion from me is when the normally wild students of Helton are standing in front of the school's display cabinets looking at sepia brown pictures of previous students. 'They were all once like you boys,' whispered the eccentric Mr Keating, played by Williams. 'But now they are all just food for worms.' He asks them to press their faces closer to the glass and listen to these old boys shout out their legacy through time. As they stand silently waiting, Mr Keating whispers in a gruff voice the Latin phrase made famous by this film, 'Carpe diem – seize the day, make your lives extraordinary.' He was teaching the boys that tomorrow is not certain so make the most of every opportunity today. Never is that truer than for a parent. You close your eyes and they are all grown up and gone, leaving you to search for precious memories and rue missed opportunities.

I can't believe that my seven-year-old son, Matthew, will one day be standing in front of a mirror shaving, or that my five-year-old Nathan will one day be sitting behind the wheel of a car driving or that my eighteen-month-old son, Joe, could one day be carrying his new bride over the threshold of their first home. As I tucked them all up in bed last night, these future thoughts seemed crazy to me. I have so many hopes and dreams for those fresh-faced little lads. I often wonder what life will be like for them when their voices are deeper and my hair is thinner. So this morning I have decided to write some of those dreams down for them to look back on one day, along with some of the biggest challenges I have faced in being their dad. I know they wouldn't fully grasp them if I tried to explain it to them today, but I hope that one day they will find this dusty old book on a shelf and read how I felt about them in the year 2003. It's a bit like burying a time capsule in the garden for them with express instructions that it not be opened until they find a bottle of hair restorer in my bathroom cabinet. So here goes . . .

Well, boys, I am writing this when Tony Blair is our Prime Minister, David Beckham the most famous footballer in the world, *EastEnders* the most watched TV programme, mobile video phone messaging the newest form of communication technology, the Harry Potter series the biggest selling books and the *Lord of the Rings* the highest grossing movie. The average wage is £22,000, the average house price is £120,000 and a loaf of bread cost about 70 pence. It is also the time when we are just about to make a big family move from Banbury, where you were all born, to Suffolk. I am sitting in my office at our home in Banbury writing this on my computer, the one you play the 'bugs' game on. You are at Bishop Loveday School being taught by Mrs Peacock and Mrs Daley. Mum is in town shopping with Joe. Soon you will all be home and I will do what I have done with you since that first day the doctor put you in my arms and I couldn't hold back the tears – I am going to squeeze you tight, lift you up, swing you round and plant a huge kiss on your cheek. I have told you that I loved you nearly every day of your life in the hope that whatever else happened, this one thing would remain constantly deep inside of you.

If 'baby' Joe is well into his teens by now, that will mean I could well be pushing sixty – if I haven't kicked the bucket that is. And now you are all grown up and reading this, you'll no doubt be thinking back to your younger days and I will be remembering back to when me and Mummy first met on a Christian youth holiday in the Lake District. It was ten years after that Matthew arrived on the scene. Mum was in labour for eighteen hours with you, Matt. By the end of it all, I was exhausted! The year previous had been the worst of our lives. Mum had had a miscarriage; you remember how we talked of Grace – the sister you never knew? I had lost my job and things were looking pretty bleak. But it was a time when we both never doubted our love for each other or God's stunningly amazing grace for us – hence, your sister's name. You guys all came along in the years that followed and although it was real hard work at times, the sheer joy and happiness you brought to us far out weighed any sleep- less nights, nasty nappies or early mornings. And so do those dreams I had for your lives . . .

Happiness was never my dream for any of you. Of course, I wanted you to be happy in life but not at any cost. A well-paid job, financial security and a big house was never my big dream for your lives. I have come to realize that as fine as those things are, they are never going to be the kind of things that mark out a fulfilled life for you. Now, I know this sounds crazy, boys, but my over-riding dream for all three of you was that by the time you left home, you were able to make good, solid life choices. My dream was always to equip you with the ability to say no to the wrong things that might seem nice and shiny at the time, and yes to the right things that aren't always that obvious at first glance. You will have found out already by now that life is full of a series of choices that need to be made every day. Some life choices are easier to make than others. Things like, Where shall I go after work tonight? How shall I spend my money? What clothes should I wear? However, some of the choices are a tough call. Things like, How far do I go to fit in? What are my criteria for choosing a vocation, a friend or a life partner? The biggest choice I ever had to make at your age was to make Jesus the leader of every part of my life. I didn't make it lightly. Your grandma and grandpa never took me to church every Sunday like we did with you. It was actually my best mate, Bernie, who first talked to me about Jesus and took me to church. That one teenage choice has proved to be the choice that feeds all the other choices in my life to this day. It is the most significant and defining choice I ever made.

So, boys, let me get specific here. Below I have listed the three top challenges I set myself as you were growing up. These are three of the most important values that I have worked at to press into your lives before you left home. How did I do? Did you realize the dream or was I way off mark? I am so aware that as a father I have had a huge influence on all your lives. Sometimes I got it badly wrong. I know that, but I hope sometimes by God's grace I got it right. I realized that if I wanted you to accept these values, I had to pass them on by what I taught you and by what you saw in my life. It was a battle because there were a lot of other people who also wanted to shape you with their values – pop stars, movie heroes, TV characters and the worst bunch of all, the advertising executives.

These values are so important to me. Many of them I learned from your grandpa as he fathered me. Just maybe you haven't bought into them as I'd hoped, but I wasn't prepared to let other people bring you up in the way you should live without my voice and my prayers being heard loud and long and often. You might not have realized it but conversations at the tea table were opportunities for me to share these values, as were our chats in the car or our reviews after watching a movie together, or our confrontations when you really wanted that toy but didn't have enough pocket money saved yet and I was too mean to buy it for you, or over a birthday burger at McDonald's, or when you had had a tough call at school, or done a great job on something or had a fight with your best friend. Trying to teach you these values was also a lot of fun. Remember when Joe was a tiny baby and we camped out in the lounge with a midnight feast when Mum was away for the weekend? I hope you never told her about that!

HOW TO MAKE IT WORK

In all I did, boys, I tried to take the Bible's parenting advice seriously: 'Point your kids in the right direction – when they're old they won't be lost' (Proverbs 22:6 MSG).

So here are the three ways in which your dad has tried to point each of you in the right direction. They are my three biggest parenting challenges for my three most precious gifts from God – Matthew, Nathan and Joe. (It must be said at this point that, without a doubt, much of my inspiration to keep 'good parenting' as a high value comes from your mum – she's good, very good, but I guess you already knew that!)

The sexual challenge

'Let her breasts satisfy thee at all times, and be thou ravished always with her love' (Proverbs 5:19 KJV).

I wanted you three boys to know that sex is brilliant and that it is one of God's best inventions. I also wanted you to be rock solid in face of sexual temptation and to make wise judgements and 'flee from sexual immorality' (1 Corinthians 6:18), because sexual temptation will come your way more often and more seductively than you imagine. You may well be very aware of that already. That's why we talked about sex openly at home and you never seemed to be embarrassed about it. When you were just seven years old, Matthew, I was kissing Mummy in the kitchen when you walked in. You saw us, turned right around and went straight out the door only to return a few minutes later with a note that you just left on the table. It simply read 'Why don't you both get naked?' Remember that? I loved the fact that we could talk so honestly about such an important life issue.

I so wanted you to grow up understanding that your sexuality was a gift from God and that the sexual feelings you have are not bad, they are a normal part of how God made you. My job was to help you understand them and to learn to express them appropriately. That's why we never had the one off 'dad and son' sex talk but an ongoing conversation that we revisited every time we saw Marge and Homer snuggling, or when you couldn't understand the meaning of some sexy lyrics you heard in a song on the radio.

At times I felt that the world was against me, but I wanted you to understand the huge value of abstinence, and how God honours us when we say no when the world keeps screaming yes. He made sex so powerful and knew that if it wasn't contained well, it would cause enormous pain and hurt. So he designed a container for it called marriage. I also wanted you to understand that the Bible doesn't say anything significant about masturbation. It obviously wasn't important enough for God to feel he had to include it. It does, however, talk about the dangers of lustful thoughts and addictive behaviour but not masturbation. I didn't want you to grow up feeling guilty so that's why I wanted you to hear the truth about these things from your dad before you heard it anywhere else.

The temper challenge

'Go ahead and be angry. You do well to be angry – but don't use your anger as a fuel for revenge. And don't stay angry. Don't go to bed angry. Don't give the devil that kind of foothold in your life' (Ephesians 4: 26-27 MSG).

Your favourite word at two, Nathan, was NO. Just like every two year old that came before you. You said no loud and you said it often. It was your standard response to our requests for you to finish your dinner, give back your brothers' toys or stop putting the cat in the tumble dryer. And your party piece was the most amazing temper tantrums. You did them so well and you always chose the most public of places for your display of rage. In Tesco's bread aisle, the front row of church on a Sunday morning and when our friends (who were the most perfect of parents) came round for dinner. I must admit that it was sometimes hilarious to watch – like a beached octopus thrashing its way out of a fisherman's net. But if we ever laughed, you would crank it up a notch.

In one way I am glad that you had such a strong ability to say no when you wanted to because when you hit the hormone years my hope was that you would still able to say a good strong NO when people offered you drugs or tempted you to get involved in dangerous relationships or activities. So when conflict came, I wanted you to be able to handle it well. When you managed to get angry and not sin, which you did achieve more often than you think, I tried to praise you, but when you became rude and hot headed, I tried to help you to manage it better. (Especially after those times when you took a tray from the kitchen and whacked it repeatedly over Matthew's head when he wouldn't let you play on the Game Boy!) I know you hated those punishments, but I didn't want bad anger management to shape your future. I wanted you to grow up to enjoy healthy relationships, not ones marred by untamed anger.

I also understood that most of what you learned about doing anger well came from how you saw me do it. I am sorry that I didn't always do it as well as I could have done. Those shouting matches didn't do either of us any good. But when we talked about it in a calm and respectful way, good learning happened. And our relationship deepened.

The spiritual challenge

'He is a God who is passionate about his relationship with you' (Exodus 34:14 NLT).

Before any of you guys were born, Mum and I were talking with some friends who had three boys who have now all grown up and left home, choosing to walk away from God. They wanted nothing to do with Jesus or his church and it broke their parents' hearts. They told us that their biggest mistake, even though they did it with the best of intentions, was to force faith into their lives from a young age. They insisted that they all went to church even when they were old enough to choose not to. They insisted that they sit at family prayers every day listening to the Bible stories over and over again and repeating family prayers. 'But wasn't that a good thing?' we asked. 'You would have thought so,' they replied, 'but it meant that when they went to church nothing was new to them, they knew it all already and it became boring to them. They grew more and more resentful the more we pursued it with them.'

So we made it our mission to let you see God at work in the everyday areas of our lives rather than to set aside religious family moments. So we never said grace – only when you asked to say it (which was surprisingly often). We never had family prayers – only when good things happened to one of us and we stopped to say thanks to God. Or when tough times came we stood together, holding hands and asked God to help us. Remember when we were trying desperately to sell our house in Banbury and you were fed up with always having to keep your rooms tidy? Nathan asked why we can't sell it quicker so he didn't have to always pack his stuff away. So we knelt on his messy bedroom floor and he prayed that God would help us sell the house and sell it soon. I had never heard such a heartfelt prayer! Or when Mummy wasn't feeling well and we stood by her bed and you prayed that God would make her better. Or when Matthew had fallen out with his best friend and he wanted to ask God to help him make it up.

The guru of the modern family is a man called Dr James Dobson. He once told a story of a little three year old who climbed up onto a chair by the front window of his house. He pulled back the huge curtains and looked at the world outside his home. His mum came into the lounge and all she could see were these two little legs poking out from under the curtain and all she could hear was a little voice sombrely repeating the phrase 'I've just got to get out of here!'

The time always comes when a child feels that way. So don't feel ashamed about the fact that you feel the need to leave home. Just maybe, boys, as you are reading this, that day has already come for one of you. My goal as your dad has been to create a home that is a place full of great memories. A place of great fun, good learning and irrational love. A place where these values have been so deeply pressed into you that nothing anyone throws at you in the future will ever shake you from it.

So that's it, boys . . . oh yes, one last promise. When you were young I always used to tickle you and I promised myself that even when you grew up I would never stop. So . . . are you still up for a bundle with your old man?

Being a good dad. I have only been a father for about eight years to date, so I am just a novice really. But here are the ten most important things I have learned so far:

1. If I routinely work more than 50 hours a week, then I will never stand a chance of being a good dad.
2. I need to continuously teach my boys everything I know, both through what I say and how I live my life.
3. Quality time is a myth.
4. I mustn't leave all the major parenting decisions to Debbie even though she spends most time with the boys. When we parent together, we grow closer together.
5. Tell the boys I love them often – especially when they don't expect it.
6. I must teach them to have a healthy respect for women (especially as in our family there are four of us boys and just one girl!).
7. It's important for me to read to them a lot and listen intently when they read to me each day.
8. It's good for me to take them into my world often and get them to meet my friends and experience some of my adventures.
9. I must try not to hide my emotions from them.
10. Bundling is great fun!

24

ARE YOUR BAGS PACKED?

How to view heaven right

NAKED LIFE

Life is full of some big questions. Here are some I am working on right now: Why is it called lipstick if you can still move your lips? Why doesn't glue stick to the inside of the bottle? Why is it that when you transport something by car it is called shipment, but when you transport something by ship it's called cargo? And why is it that when you are driving and looking for an address, you always turn the radio down? And why is lemon juice made with artificial flavours and yet dishwashing liquid is made with real lemons? How do you get off a non-stop flight? And how can there be self-help 'groups'? And if they make tin whistles out of tin, what do they make foghorns out of? And, of course the ultimate question, Why didn't Noah swat those two mosquitoes? Yes, I know what you are thinking now: those long winter evenings must just fly by in our house! (Ooh . . . I've just thought of another: if swimming is so good for you, then why do whales look the way they do?)

But when it comes down to it, man's biggest question is, and always will be, What happens when I die? Problem is, you are not really supposed to say the 'D' word in this day and age. So no one often airs the question in public or finds an answer. It's as frowned upon today as much as the 'S' word was 50 years ago. A good example of our phobia is *life* insurance. By rights, it should really be called *death* insurance because it only gets paid out when we die! It's just that we can't mention *that* word. Why is death such a taboo subject? Has the word *death*, as Os Guinness once said, really become the new pornography?

But how can we talk about making life work without facing the reality of death? After all, it's a part of life and it is the ultimate statistic – one out of every one person dies. No amount of anti-wrinkle cream or Botox injections will keep it at bay forever. And no amount of visiting our Internet death clock will tell us the exact date to expect its call. Benjamin Franklin wittily summed this up when he said, 'There is nothing so certain in life as death . . . and taxes!'

A newspaper recently reported the story of an Illinois man who left the snow-filled streets of Chicago for a vacation in the Florida sunshine. His wife was on a business trip and was planning to meet him in Florida the next day. When he reached his hotel, he decided to send his wife a quick email. Unable to find the scrap of paper he had written her email address on, he did his best to type it from memory. Unfortunately, he missed out one letter and his note was instead directed to an elderly minister's wife whose husband had passed away the day before. When the grieving widow checked her email, she took one look at the monitor, let out a piercing scream and fell to the floor in a dead faint. At the sound, her family rushed into the room and saw this note on her screen:

Dearest wife:
Just got checked in. Everything prepared for your arrival tomorrow.
P.S. Sure is hot down here . . .

As surely as you hold this book in your hand, death will one day come your way. So are you prepared for your arrival – whenever that may be? My great friend Doug told me how he got a call from his ageing mum one Sunday afternoon. She was coming to stay and she had rung to say she was ready for him to pick her up.

'My bags are packed and I'm ready to go, son.'

Those were her last words. Doug arrived to find her slumped by the phone next to her packed bags. Are you ready for the inevitable? Or does death grip you with a fear that is ruining life? Does the thought of your future life beyond the grave fill you with hope or dread? Can we ever be sure that we will find life after death?

One man who was packed and ready to go was the author and minister David Watson. He died in 1985 of cancer at only fifty years of age yet was able to say, 'When I die it is my firm conviction that I shall be more alive than ever, experiencing the full reality of all that God has prepared for me in Jesus.'

You too can have that same firm conviction. Maybe you have never thought about death much before. Maybe you think you are too young, too fit or too busy. Just maybe you need to begin to get a fresh perspective.

The best way to find wisdom for making your life work is to be real about the subject of death. Moses wrote, 'Teach us to use wisely all the time we have' (Psalm 90:12 CEV).

The Bible also says we are to remember that we are just passing through in this life. We are like refugees, strangers and visitors in a foreign country: 'I am but a pilgrim here on earth: how I need a map' (Psalm 119:19 TLB).

So don't get too comfy down here because you are not going to be here for long. You are just a visitor. In fact, Jesus said that he has already gone to prepare your real home in heaven for your arrival. 'If that weren't so, would I have told you that I'm on my way to get a room ready for you? . . . I'll come back and get you so you can live where I live' (John 14:2–3 MSG).

HOW TO MAKE IT WORK

I often wonder what my heavenly room will be like? Will it be en-suite? Will it have a Sky TV? Will it be next to Cliff Richard? There are so many myths and legends about heaven and eternity. So let me fill you again with some real hope and blow away some of those unhelpful Sunday school myths. These three truths below are designed to cement hope back into your heart as you contemplate your life beyond the grave.

Myth 1: Heaven will be about as much fun as watching re-runs of the weather channel (and you can't find the remote)

'What God has planned for people who love him is more than eyes have seen or ears have heard. It has never even entered our minds' (1 Corinthians 2:9 CEV).

I used to really worry about heaven. I thought it would be one long church service with dusty old songs, tunes as dull as my dad's record collection and words as incomprehensible as a physics text-book . . . written in the original Greek! And I would be made to sing in the choir. The seats would be hard, the sermons boring and the tea tasteless. And worst of all, it would go on forever and ever and ever. Unlike the children's movie *The Never-Ending Story*, this one really would be never-ending – no final scene, no closing credits and no escape.

The truth is, you will be fit to burst with so much joy on that day that you won't be able to stop yourself singing. A joy that comes from finally meeting this Jesus. This Jesus who you have followed, sung about and prayed to on this earth – you will meet him face-to-face.

Try picturing you, ordinary you, in heaven, face-to-face with Jesus. Mind blowing, isn't it? In fact, it's so wild Paul says it has never even entered our minds. You could commission the greatest songwriters ever to capture the essence of heaven and they wouldn't come close. You could employ the most creative film directors of the century to write *Heaven: The Movie* and they wouldn't get past the opening credits. You could ask J.K. Rowling to write a new best-selling book that replaces Hogwarts with heaven, and even she wouldn't know where to begin. It's more than eyes have seen, ears have heard or minds have ever conceived and you know what? It's waiting for you and, unlike your most memorable holiday ever, it will never have a last day. You'll never have to catch a return flight because you will be home already. Myth says heaven will be boring; truth says you will never know such joy as on that day. Doesn't that fill you with hope?

Myth 2: Heaven will be full of white, middle class westerners having one big long Christian conference (and my seat is bound to be front row, centre)

Heaven: scene one

'*So at the name of Jesus everyone will bow down, those in heaven, on earth, and under the earth. And to the glory of God the father everyone will openly agree, "Jesus Christ is Lord!"*' (Philippians 2:10–11 CEV).

Let's remember that a day is coming when every knee will bow before Jesus – not just your knees or my knees, but everyone's knees. Even those knees that find it tough to bow today will have to bow to Jesus on that day. The highest paid movie star, the most powerful politician, the most influential business leader, the most photographed sports star – they will all have to bend their knees, however reluctantly. And they will find themselves bowing in front of those who once bowed before them. There will be no distinction. Black knees will bow next to white knees, rich will bow beside the poor, oppressor will bow with the oppressed. And those who couldn't find fairness in this world will find God's fairness pouring all over them.

Heaven: scene two

'I looked again. I saw a huge crowd, too huge to count. Everyone was there – all nations and tribes, all races and languages. And they were ... standing before the Throne ... and heartily singing' (Revelation 7:9–10 MSG).

The apostle John points out that believers from every nation, every tribe, every tongue will stand and worship God on that day. Can you imagine what it will be like on that day? A day that will herald a peace that won't ever break down or need policing. No more terrorist bombs and no more government sanctions; no more Catholic snipers and no more Protestant beatings; no more Palestinian suicide bombers and no more Israeli tank raids.

Myth says heaven is just for the middle classes; truth says we will one day be surprised at who is there bowing the knee and even more surprised at who isn't. Doesn't a heaven flowing with mutual respect and love for everybody fill you with hope?

Myth 3: I will still feel like hell even if I am in heaven (and it will go on hurting forever just like it does down here)

'He'll wipe every tear from their eyes. Death is gone for good – tears gone, crying gone, pain gone – all the first order of things gone' (Revelation 21:3 MSG).

Here's the ultimate hope. I know you hurt right now. I know the tears sting as you cry yourself to sleep at night. I have been there in life and will probably be there again. But let me remind you once again: You are not home yet. You may well be feeling a little homesick and that's no bad thing, because ready for you is a home with no doctor's waiting rooms since you won't be sick – ever. And with no psychiatrists to talk with because you won't be depressed – ever! And with no funeral homes to visit because you won't grieve – ever.

Please understand me. These are not my words or my clever thoughts. This is not some writer's myth – it's true. The Bible promises it and it's been the hope of Christians for thousands of years. Jesus is the only person ever to face death and come out the other side. What better person can you find to be your guide when you come to walk through that door? How can people say no to a hope like this?

The writer Max Lucado ends his book *Travelling Light* with this paragraph of hope for those of us in pain on earth.

> And when you see him, you'll set [your luggage] down. Just as a returning soldier drops his duffel when he sees his wife, you'll drop everything when you see your father. Those you love will shout. Those you know will applaud. But all the noise will cease when he cups your chin and says, 'Welcome home.' And with scarred hand he'll wipe every tear from your eye. And you will dwell in the house of the Lord – forever.

Myth says the pain will go on in heaven. Truth says tears gone, crying gone, pain gone! Is that your hope today?

Heaven. Picture the scene at my house right now. It's Monday morning, 10.30. The deadline for this book is looming ever larger like a huge freight train on the horizon. My two eldest boys are at school and my wife is asleep upstairs (she worked a 12-hour shift at the hospital last night). I am attempting to work on the couch with my laptop resting on my . . . well, on my lap! To my left is Buzz Light Year who occasionally reminds me that he wants to go beyond infinity but never does anything about this conviction. To my right is Joe, my one-year-old. He has spent the last 20 minutes drinking water from his beaker whilst attempting to hit Varrrrrrious keyssss o4n the

comutor —- an ruin ALAL my HARDwork////. However, his eyes
have now become droopy and he has slumped into what looks like a
very uncomfortable position with his head wedged under a cushion.
He looks so cute, but when I have finished this paragraph I am going
to pick him up and carry him upstairs to bed. It's time for him to rest
and it's going to be much better for him to rest upstairs than it is down
here.

I get to wonder if that is how our heavenly Father views death.
After all, won't he also one day carry us up to a place of rest when we
finally fall asleep? Because he knows that up there is a far better place
for us to be. You see, death is not the ultimate tragedy to his children.
It might well be that our bodies are finished but in reality our life is
only just beginning. One day Jesus will say to you, 'Come, you who
are blessed by my Father; take your inheritance, the kingdom prepared for you since the creation of the world' (Matthew 25:34). Can't
wait . . .

25

STAY THE COURSE (THE MOST IMPORTANT LESSON OF ALL)

How to beat the temptation to quit

NAKED LIFE

I love this little story. It warms your heart . . .

A little old couple walked slowly into McDonald's one cold winter's evening. They looked out of place amid the young families and young couples eating there that night. Some of the customers looked admiringly at them. You could tell what the admirers were thinking: *Look, there is a couple who have been through a lot together, probably for sixty years or more!* The old man walked right up to the cash register, placed his order with no hesitation and then paid for their meal.

The couple took a table near the back wall and started taking food off of the tray. There was one hamburger, one order of fries and one drink. The little old man unwrapped the plain hamburger and carefully cut in half. He placed one half in front of his wife. Then he carefully counted out the fries, divided them into two piles and neatly placed one pile in front of his wife. He took a sip of the drink, his wife took a sip and then set the cup down between them.

As the man began to eat his few bites of hamburger, the crowd began to get restless. Again you could tell what they were thinking: That poor old couple. All they can afford is one meal for the two of them. As the man began to eat his fries, one young man stood and came over to the old couple's table. He politely offered to buy another meal for the old couple to eat. The old man replied that they were just fine. They were used to sharing everything.

Then the crowd noticed that the little old lady hadn't eaten a bite. She just sat there watching her husband eat and occasionally taking turns sipping the drink. Again the young man came over and begged them to let him buy them something to eat. This time the lady explained that they were used to sharing everything together.

As the little old man finished eating and was wiping his face neatly with a napkin, the young man could stand it no longer. Again he came over to their table and offered to buy some food. After being politely refused again, he finally asked the question of the little old lady: 'Ma'am, why aren't you eating? You said you share everything. What is it that you are waiting for?'

She answered, 'The teeth.'

But what is it that you are waiting for before you bite fully into life and let its juices run down your cheek? Is it just that life is tough and you don't know if you have got the energy left to pursue it anymore? Is it that your greatest ambitions never get realized?

Well, let me give you some teeth. But you need to remember that it's not going to be an easy ride. As Paul says:

> We've been surrounded and battered by troubles, but we're not demoralized; we're not sure what to do, but we know that God knows what to do; we've been spiritually terrorized, but God hasn't left our side; we've been thrown down, but we haven't broken (2 Corinthians 4:8–9 MSG).

How can Paul say all that 'not demoralized' stuff after being surrounded, battered, thrown down and terrorized? One word sums it up: *perseverance*. He kept on going to the end. Watch a Grand Prix, or a steeplechase or a marathon and the winner is not the one who necessarily starts the best but who keeps on going to the end. It's the essential quality for any who wish to squeeze every last drop out of life. Problem is, you can't microwave perseverance.

So, how do we stay the course?

I have read back through all I have written in this book and am more convinced than ever that I don't want to spend my life just working, I want to make my one time shot at life work – really work.

For over 198 pages I have talked about real life and made some suggestions as to how to make it work. I have given you my twenty-five best thoughts on improving your relationship with God and others, on growing old, on getting the best from your work, your money, your body, your time and your leisure activities. And what's best of all is that the principles I have outlined are based on the bedrock of God's Word so they will stand the test of time. But here's the sting in the tail. (You may want to be sitting down at this point.) You can't do it – it's impossible. I know that's hard to stomach but before you rush off to St Agatha's Under-the-Hill Christian Bookshop demanding your money back, here's the good news.

God knows it's impossible for you so he promises to work with you in the business of making life work. It's a joint effort – a partnership, because self help is an oxymoron. Your part of the deal is to make him the leader of your life; his is to give you all the power and enthusiasm you need to persevere to the end. Sounds like a win-win proposition to me.

Let me explain this 'you and God' partnership in life from the Bible.

God's part of the deal: 'There has never been the slightest doubt in my mind that the God who started this great work in you would keep at it and bring it to a flourishing finish' (Philippians 1:6 MSG).

You're part of the deal: 'Better yet, redouble your efforts. Be energetic in your life of salvation' (Philippians 2:12 MSG).

The result of the deal: 'And so we are transfigured much like the Messiah, our lives becoming brighter and more beautiful as God enters our lives and we become like him' (2 Corinthians 3:18 MSG).

It's a bit like this: You are flying away on your summer holidays. You've got your factor 25 in one hand and your Dick Francis in the other. Your ticket says you are on the 11 a.m. flight, in row 6 seat D (invariably right between the screaming child and the *Star Trek* fan). You are to arrive two hours prior to boarding so you can check your bags in. You notice some mistletoe hanging over the baggage counter. The clerk informs you that this is the place where you kiss your luggage goodbye. Now you can head off into the terminal building to spend a promiscuous amount of money on a coffee and an out-of-date sesame seed muffin drizzled with warm battery acid. Eventually you are told to walk to gate 64 (which is in another time zone) where you are then instructed to board the plane in seat order. Once seated you are to concentrate on the stewards' cheery mime for the crash landing procedure and then read the safety card in the seat pocket in front of you. A small light above your head 'pings' you an instruction to fasten your seatbelt for your safety. (You wonder why soon you will be at 50,000 feet and allowed to roam freely around the plane, but when you are on the ground travelling at 1 mph you are told to sit down and put your seatbelt on!)

At last you are ready to go. You have fulfilled your part of the bargain. You have done all you can. There is nothing more you can do to get you to your destination. You have obeyed the instructions on your ticket and all you can do now is sit back, relax and enjoy the flight. Now you must move from simple obedience to complete trust. Only the pilot can get you off the ground and on your way. Only he can move the plane towards its destination. He can't take you if you don't obey the instructions, and you can't go unless you buckle up and trust him to get you there. It's a partnership – a joint effort. As we obey the maker's instructions, he provides the power for the engines and the direction for the journey.

HOW TO MAKE IT WORK

So here they are, my final three best thoughts on obeying the pilot's instructions. They are the ABC's of persevering to the finish. Your job is to buckle them up safely into your life, and God will give you the power to persevere all the way to the end. Chocks away . . .

A – Aim for attitude and character above anything else

Attitude: 'Your attitude should be the same as that of Christ Jesus' (Philippians 2:5).

How important is the attitude you carry in life? Author Charles Swindoll tells us in black and white in his best-selling book *Improving Your Serve:*

> The longer I live, the more I realize the impact of attitude on life. Attitude, to me, is more important than facts. It's more important than the past. Than education, than money, than circumstances than failures, than successes, than what other people think or say or do. It is more important than appearances, giftedness, or skill. It will make or break a company, a church, or a home. The remarkable thing is that we have a choice everyday regarding the attitude we will embrace for the day. We cannot change our past. Nor can we change the inevitable. The only thing that we can do is play on the one string we have, and that is our attitude. I am convinced that life is 10 percent what happens to me and 90 percent how I react to it. And so it is with you – we are in charge of our attitudes.

Your attitude to people and situations that are part of your everyday world will determine how you handle both your feelings and actions towards them. There is no doubt that your feelings will sometimes be good and sometimes bad. And that's okay but your attitude will shape how you handle those feelings. A car cuts you up, a colleague puts you down, a partner cheats on you or a friend lies to you. It's at those times that your feelings of anger and upset come to the

surface. It's then that you have an attitude choice – negative or positive. Your attitude will then determine your actions. As Swindoll
says, you can't change the inevitable but you can play on the one
string you have – attitude!

Character: *'And endurance builds character, which gives us a hope'*
(Romans 5:4 CEV).

How important is the character you develop in life? It's been said
that character is simply a long habit continued. The great evangelist
D.L. Moody was once asked which people gave him the most trouble
in everyday life. His answer was brilliant: 'I've more trouble with D.L.
Moody than with any man alive.'

What are you really made of? That's the big character question
we all need to find an answer to at some point in our lives. A good
friend of mine was away from home on business. He told me how,
during some free time, he got himself into a major character dilemma.
He found himself alone in a seedy back-street shop with a porno magazine in his hand. As he rummaged around in his pocket for his
money, he wrestled in his mind with his actions: *No one will know this
far from home, I can always ask God to forgive me, and I deserve some
self-gratification*. He got himself as far as placing the book on the
counter in order for the assistant to take his money and put it in its
brown paper cover when he made the right character choice, apolo-
gized and got out. 'I found myself running out of the shop,' he told me
'and back to the hotel. In my room I took out the picture of my wife
and kids, feeling glad that when I get home to see them again I will
feel clean inside.'

The word *character* is almost indefinable. Ask most people to
define it, and they end up describing a person who they admire who
knows how to do the right things in life.

Another man who had a similar character dilemma as my friend
was Joseph. He grew his character early in life when his brothers

turned against him. As this boy became a man, it gave him the strength to cope with the corruption of Pharaoh's palace life. This integrity of character meant that Joseph quickly rose to a place of great influence but like my pastor friend, he found himself in a compromising situation with Potiphar's wife who had been chatting him up every day. Eventually she invited him to jump in the sack with her (Genesis 39:7). He said no but his refusal got him thrown in jail. God was with him in the prison and the brightness of his character even won favour with the guards. Eventually he was restored to his former position and Pharaoh said to others about him, 'Can we find anyone like this man, one in whom is the spirit of God?' (Genesis 41:38).

It was this life-long, uncompromising, wise character choice of right from wrong that made Joseph the kind of person I long to be. Today is not too late to get yourself squared off with God and get back on the path to good character development. And who knows what kind of influential position you just might find yourself in.

Here are three simple ways to kick-start your character development:

1. Don't run from the hard times – they are the best character developers.
2. Take 31 days to read the 31 chapters of Proverbs. (I have found the CEV Bible the best to do this with.) Billy Graham is said to have lived in the proverbs. If it's good enough for Billy . . .
3. Find an honest friend. You'll never do it on your own. Get a character-growing buddy and be brutally honest with each other!

B – Become a child again and colour outside the lines

'*Mark this: Unless you accept God's kingdom in the simplicity of a child, you'll never get it*' (Mark 10:15 MSG).

A man asked his wife, 'What would you most like for your birthday?' She answered, 'I'd love to be ten again.'

On the morning of her birthday, he got up bright and early and off they went to a theme park. He put her on every ride in the park – the Death Slide, the Screaming Loop, the Wall of Fear. She had a go on everything there. She staggered out of the theme park five hours later, her head reeling and her stomach upside down. Next they went into McDonald's, where she was given a Double Big Mac with extra fries and a strawberry shake. Then it was off to the movies to see *Star Wars* accompanied by more burgers, popcorn, coke and sweets.

At last she staggered home with her husband and collapsed into bed. He leaned over to her tenderly and asked, 'Well darling, what was it like being ten again?'

With one eye opened she groaned, 'Actually I meant dress size!'

Jesus said that unless we become childlike again in our understanding of faith, then we have no chance of finding authentic kingdom life. We need to learn to re-imagine the sheer exhilaration of being a child and apply it to our relationship with God.

Mike Yaconelli in his book *Dangerous Wonder* laments:

> Somewhere along the way we [have] had the child chased out of us . . . childlike faith is faith that trusts Jesus' standard of living (seek first the kingdom of God) instead of society's standard of living (seek first the kingdom of things).

Living well will mean doing some childlike kingdom activities and you are never too old to begin. A sign at the start of a long dusty road that goes for miles across the barren Australian outback reads: 'Choose your rut carefully. You'll be in it for the next 200 miles'.

Don't let your life gather dust. I met a lovely lady in a coffee shop yesterday. We got talking in the cappuccino queue. She was retired, her beloved Fred passed on some years ago. Thinking how tough life must be for her, I asked how she was managing.

'I am having the time of my life. At my age you have to grab life by the collar and shake the best bits out of it. I do amateur dramatics two nights a week – I am in the chorus of My *Fair Lady* tonight. Do you want a ticket? I do hospital visits most days and I am on the committee for the W.I. Oh ... and next week I am flying out to the Far East to visit my son. How about you young man?'

My sensible grown-up rut didn't seem to match up somehow, so I coughed nervously and bought her a large latte.

Don't ask if God will catch you if you jump off the top step into his arms – just jump. Don't ask what others might think if you get excited in worship – just dance. Don't hold back the tears if emotion strikes – just cry. And you don't have to stay with that sensible career when your heart is somewhere else – just breakout and find a new adventure in God's kingdom. Max Lucado writes in his book *He Still Moves Stones*:

> Life has rawness and wonder. Pursue it. Hunt for it. Don't listen to the whines of those who have settled for a second rate life and want you to do the same. Your goal is not to live long; it's to live. Jesus says the options are clear. To be safe, you can build a fire in the hearth, stay inside, and keep warm and dry. You can't get hurt if you never get out, right? You can't be criticized for what you don't try, right? You can't fail if you don't take a stand, right?.... So don't try it. Take the safe route.

Instead of building a fire in your hearth, however, you can build a fire in your heart. Follow God's impulses. Adopt a child. Move overseas. Teach a class. Change careers. Run for office. Make a difference. Sure it isn't safe, but what is? You think staying inside is safe? Jesus disagrees: 'Whoever wants to save his own life will lose it' (Matthew 16:25). Reclaim the curiosity of your childhood. Just because you are near the top of the hill doesn't mean you've passed your peak.

C – Cultivate the disciplines and find freedom

'Exercise daily in God – no spiritual flabbiness, please! Workouts in the gymnasium are useful, but a disciplined life in God is far more so, making you fit both today and forever' (1 Timothy 4:8 MSG).

The world is getting smaller. Living in our global village means that companies are increasingly keen to exploit international markets. But many of them are finding it hard to crack cultural and language differences. For example, the Scandinavian vacuum manufacturer Electrolux used the following in an American ad campaign: 'Nothing Sucks Like an Electrolux'. And in Taiwan, the translation of Pepsi slogan 'Come Alive with the Pepsi Generation' came out as 'Pepsi Will Bring Your Ancestors Back from the Dead'.

For the Christ-follower, there can often be a big gap between what God says and what we experience. He promises to be with us always, to give us the power to overcome any temptation and to fill us with Holy Spirit joy. The problem is there is often a gap between what is promised and what actually happens in our lives. So some people fake faith or just quit all together. If we are going to last for the long haul, we are going to have to find ways of closing that gap. The key element is not rocket science. Paul's advice to Timothy is as valid today as it was 2000 years ago – exercise daily in God.

Bill Hybels writes,

I am a little embarrassed to admit this, but the truth about me is that if I do not set aside a time for a private meeting with God at least once in every twenty-four hours, I tend to drift way off course spiritually. Instead of devoting myself to God's agenda, I become consumed with my own agenda. Instead of being sensitive to people around me, I become insensitive. Instead of trying to work out how to be a greater servant of my congregation, I start working out manipulative ways to get other people to do my bidding. And it only takes two or three days of missing meetings with God to put me in that serious condition.

The daily discipline of meeting with God is the key to closing the gap between what we know of his promises and what really happens in our lives. Just as a champion athlete can't escape the daily discipline of physical training, the winning Christian can't escape the daily discipline of spiritual training. Silence, study, celebration, serving, fasting, solitude – these kinds of disciplines create space for God's spirit to fill our minds and transform our lives. Dallas Willard describes them as simple acts that interrupt the normal flow of our habitual daily thinking. And I want to remind you that, without a doubt, the rewards are definitely worth the effort.

In the book *The Collection*, Richard Foster tells of his dilemma as he was researching his best-selling book on spiritual disciplines called *Finding the Heart's True Home*.

> Over those months, I suppose I worked my way through 300 or so books in the field of prayer – classical books and contemporary books. Books, books, books. My head was just swimming with all the debates about prayer, all of the divisions of prayer, all the discussions and definitions of prayer ... At one time, I had identified 41 major forms of prayer in the great devotional writers ... I'll never forget a night in July 1990. There I was in that library all alone. Everybody had left hours before. I had studied too much, it was too late and I had worked too hard. How could anybody deal with all of the intricacies and difficulties of prayer in one book? I threw my hands up ready to abandon the project.
>
> Then something happened to me that is hard for me to express to you ... As best as I can discern it, I heard the voice of the true Shepherd, not outwardly but inwardly saying:
>
> 'I don't want you to abandon the project. Instead, I want you to tell my children that my heart is broken. Tell them I hurt at their distance and their pre-occupation. Tell them I mourn that they do not draw near to me. Tell them I grieve that they have forgotten me. Tell them I weep over their obsession with muchness and manyness. Tell them that I long for their presence.'

No matter how you might be feeling, God is desperate for your presence. It really doesn't matter what you have done or what you have
not done. It's of no consequence to him how long it has been since you
have talked to him. Today is a new day. And as you make that daily
sacrifice of coming to him in prayer, you will once again know intimacy and wholeness; forgiveness and acceptance; love and affirmation.
You will find your spiritual muscles developing and your spiritual stam-
ina growing deeper. Then you will see the gap closing between the life
God promises you and the life you experience every day.

Keep going. I once heard someone describe our life with God as that
of a surfer. It takes a lot of hard work and training to surf well. Then
when you are on the board, you are not just simply taken for a ride.
You have to hold on tight, keep your feet in the right position and
keep the sail pointing into the wind. But the one thing you can't do
is make the wave. That's God's job. It's his pleasure to lift you and
move you and thrill you with the adventure of life's highs and lows.
And when you fall off, you find another wave coming along right
behind. His power in your life is not some odd wave that washes up
on the beach every now and again. They keep coming again and
again and again – look, there's another one just coming now.

If you keep in mind what I have told you the Lord
will help you understand completely.

2 TIMOTHY 2:7 CEV